SINGAPORE · MALAYSIA

CULTURE SHOCK!

JoAnn Craig

Times Books International
Singapore

Cover design by Karen Hoisington
Cartoons by Arthero
Cover cartoon by Sam Rawi

© **1979 Times Books International**
Times Centre, 1 New Industrial Road
Singapore 1953

Reprinted 1979, 1980, 1981,
1982, 1984

Revised Edition 1986

Printed by Khai Wah Printers, Singapore

ISBN 9971 65 341 9

To Joe, David, Erik, Kenny, Jim, Raj, Bhopinder, Keng, Nick, Len, Mano, Harry, Jai and Chiew Seen Kong . . . and to Lynn, Leslie, Suzie, Patty, Juanita, Bibijon, Tina, Yogi, Rani, Neela, Kathi and Sunghee . . . and all the other young people of the world, in the hope that the new generation will grow in mutual love and respect for each other's cultures

Contents

3
THE CHINESE COMMUNITY

Foreword

JoAnn modestly believes that I can express her objectives in writing this book better than she can, a belief with which I could quibble—but in fact, I am only too delighted to have my name associated with this book, which I regard as a splendid and essential piece of cultural bridge-work.

I hope that JoAnn's constant eagerness to learn about, and to love, her environment, whatever it may be, will serve as an example to all visitors—tourists or expatriates—as well as members of the different ethnic communities who may not be familiar with each other's customs.

JoAnn is fully aware that this is not a definitive book and there may indeed be the occasional mistake, easily made in as complex and plural a society as ours, where the older generation is in any case far more faithful to traditional Asian mores than the young.

She can also foresee that she will very likely attract the jibe of being "patronising" from locals as well as tourists and expatriates who love to carp and moan instead of getting on with work like JoAnn's themselves.

None of this deters her from her main objective which is, quite simply, "to get more people to love and understand each other". And she is understandably irritated, as I myself am, with the cultural myopia evinced by those who look once at the skyscraper skyline in the cities, the sophisticated lifestyle and polished public English, and then conclude there is nothing Asian about Singapore and Malaysia. Skyscrapers, however, in my opinion, and in JoAnn's, are only skin-deep—to penetrate deeper, you need the help that people like JoAnn are able to give you.

This is just the beginning—JoAnn hopes to continue her practical anthropological studies and hopes that others will follow in her footsteps. I myself am very pleased to have had a hand in transforming this "ivory tower" university paper into a practical handbook for newcomers to Singapore and Malaysia.

Just one last word of caution: this book is not meant to complicate your life or to subject you to the social strain of constantly wondering if you have culturally put your foot in it! When in doubt, relax, listen, be friendly and be yourself—for most Singaporeans and Malaysians, that will be quite enough, and will conform to the dominant tenets of their own lifestyle.

Ilsa Sharp
Singapore 1978

Introduction

The society of Singapore and Malaysia is a plural society comprising a multi-lingual, multi-ethnic and multi-religious people. These people have created a new society in which different ethnic groups have blended together to become one people; yet each group has retained its own special uniqueness and individuality which add to the special charm and exotic flavour of these countries.

In many ways the local customs and courtesies are different from the traditional good manners of a Western culture. We tend to think that basic good manners and etiquette are universally understood and practised in the same way; we may not realise that what constitutes good manners in one society may have exactly the opposite effect in another. In fact, Western etiquette may be offensive or even insulting in an Eastern culture! This book is written in the hope that it will help people from a Western cultural background to develop a deeper understanding of, and better interpersonal relationships with, people of an Eastern culture. The rules of social etiquette in *any* society are difficult to classify, and this is even more so in Singapore and Malaysia where there are three major social groups with diverse forms of social etiquette: Chinese, Indian, and Malay.

Good manners are really the basic consideration for the feelings of another person. If we care about someone, we try to understand his customs, etiquette, local courtesies, and the rules that regulate the conduct of his daily life. This is one of the best ways of establishing a basis for friendship and cooperation. This does not mean that we must relinquish our own standards of manners, values, beliefs and attitudes; we need only expand them in the name of friendship and goodwill.

In a Western culture, it is good manners to walk into someone's home with your shoes on (it would be considered rude to remove them!), it is considered friendly to shake hands with all people of both sexes whom we meet; it is permissible to give objects with either hand; it is often a normal social friendliness to hug or kiss the host or hostess when entering or leaving their home; it is considered thoughtful to serve a juicy steak to special guests; it is acceptable to gesture to a person or a taxi with the forefinger pointed out and waving. But in Singapore and Malaysia all these customs are taboo in one or more of the different ethnic groups.

The people of Singapore and Malaysia are a kind and courteous people. They are tolerant and understanding of the breaches we make in social etiquette. They realise, more than we do, that we have basic cultural differences and thus express ourselves differently. They hesitate to embarrass us by telling us that we have committed some social blunder, or that we have put our cultural foot in our mouth. On the other hand, we as Westerners are visitors in this country, and it would be appropriate on our part if we polished up our image by showing an interest in, and concern for, the customs, manners, and local courtesies of our host country.

Sometimes we may feel that something is not going well, that our message does not seem to be getting across, that a misunderstanding has occurred and we do not know why. We find that major behavioural cues are being missed and that assumptions on one side of an interaction are not being met by the other side. This is commonly known as "culture shock" (more on this later); it is experienced by most travellers, tourists and expatriates when visiting or living in a foreign country. While trying to signal friendship, we may be: touching when we should not be touching; wearing shorts when we should be covered up; inadvertently making "obscene" gestures in front of our host's wife and children; offering gifts that are associated with death and funerals and communicating distress rather than joy; and patting a child's head without realising that many prayers will be necessary to remove the bad luck associated with that gesture. A person in "culture shock" often does not realise why things are going wrong, but at times like these he is aware that culture is very real and that all people are not bound by universal patterns of understanding.

This book is written in the hope that it will lead to better relationships between the people of Eastern and Western cultures. The information presented here reflects the unique etiquette of Singapore and Malaysia: the way the people treat each other, and the way they wish to be treated—with thoughtfulness and respect. These courtesies and considerations help to form the basis of their everyday pattern of living.

Due to the lack of written material available, I have relied on oral interviews for most of the information presented here. Some important customs may have been left out, or others may have been misrepresented. For any errors or omissions, I apologise. I also confess to being subjective.

Aside from the etiquette of Singapore and Malaysia, I have added some items of cultural interest to help the tourist, the visitor and the expatriate get a feel for the people of this society. The tourist may not always have the opportunity to meet and mix with the local people : if he misses this, then he has missed the best part of these countries!

I have also given some information on the important passages in a person's life, i.e., courtship, puberty, engagement, marriage, birth and death. These are the times when Westerners are mostly likely to interact with local friends and neighbours. A description of the rite or ritual is followed by the etiquette, etc., that is appropriate for the occasion.

I have not spoken about festivals (except for the Chinese New Year and Indian Thaipusam festivals), as there are many fine books available that explain them more fully and beautifully than I am able to do in this book.

All people are the same . . . it's only their habits that are so different!
Confucius

Acknowledgements

I would like to comment on the cooperation and kindness shown to me by Singaporeans and Malaysians in taking the time to explain their local customs and courtesies to me. This knowledge was also served with tea and cakes, curries and drinks, good fun and good talk. It has been an unforgettable experience for me, and one that I value.

I would like to say thank you especially to Mr C.M. Wong of the China Society of Singapore for showing me the humorous heart of the Chinese.

To Mr Chen Heng Wing, thank you for explaining the intricacies of Chinese dining and the pleasures of the Chinese cuisine.

To Mr Lim Kim Guan, Singapore tourist guide, Cikgu Ehsan Haji Ali, beloved "father" to countless high-school students at the Singapore American School for over 25 years, and Mr V.T. Arasu of the Ministry of Culture . . . I am very grateful for all the hours you have spent teaching, explaining and clarifying the customs and culture of Singapore to me. Also, thank you for spending days, and even weeks, in checking my information.

To my classmates at the University of Singapore, thank you all for listening to me talk . . . and talk . . . and talk some more on this topic, and thank you for all your help and suggestions. I am especially grateful to: Mr Bhopinder Singh, Mr Raj Kumar, Mr Jai Chandra, Miss Juanita Narona, Mr A. Mani, Mr Isa bin Hassan, M. Hussein Mutalib, Joyce Tan, Lee Nyuk Har, Miss Yogi Yogarajah, Miss Asiah Harun, Miss Jayarani Pavadarayan, and Miss Nila Ibrahim.

To the countless other people whom I interviewed, thank you for giving me your time and taking the trouble to help me put together this book. I am indebted to you all, but especially to: Miss Jalaja Menon, Mrs J. Verma, Mr Yang Mohsin bin Abdul Rashid, Mr Koh Ding Chiang, Sukianh binte Abu, Radiah binté Suri, Gan Siew Tin, Sharuddin bin Suri and some of the staff of the American Embassy, Information Office.

I am very grateful to those who allowed me to use their photographs in this book and to those friends who contributed photographs.

To my dear friends, Cikgu Abduhl Ghani and his family of Bachok, Malaysia, thank you for the happy talk and the happy days spent in your village. I won't forget you and all that you taught me!

To Michael A.H.B. Walter, my Anthropology teacher at the University of Singapore, thank you for your support, but most of all thank you for the example you set for all of us in respect and appreciation for the multi-ethnic people of Singapore and Malaysia.

To the man who taught me to love Anthropology, Professor David Hammond-Tooke, of the University of Witswatersrand, South Africa . . . thank you, my friend.

To Chiew Seen Kong, the man who opens the minds of the young students at the University of Singapore (and some of the older ones as well), thank you for opening mine!

To Captain A.P. "Flip" Johnson of Garuda Airlines, thank you for helping me with the most difficult part of work of this kind, i.e., framing the questions rather than finding the answers!

To Roy Ruderman of C.B.I. Overseas Inc., thank you for your patient reading and rereading, and for your constant (constructive) criticism! Thank you especially for your support.

I have a special debt to Ilsa Sharp for all the encouragement she gave, the foreword, and also for brainstorming the title of this book. Thank you, Ilsa.

To Robert C. Cooper, my teacher in Anthropology at the University of Singapore, thank you for taking me by the hand and leading me gently through the maze of academia. Also, my heartfelt thanks for *posing* as the "Ugly Expat" opposite page 1. Those who know and love you are aware that it is only a pose; to all others I would like to point out that you are a good and kind man and would never think of acting that way in real life!

To Mr Zeke Feuerman, of Pratt and Whitney, my beautiful "Ugly Expat" on page 10—I really did hate to portray you in the midst of a cultural gaff, as you and Zinna are two of the most "Cosmopolitan Expats" I've ever had the pleasure to love. Thanks for all your help and advice.

To Mead Scofield, Joe and Patty Craig, Kevin Stein, Kevin Ching, Jim Langham, Mike Zenker, John Ahmed, Sunghee Kim, Danny Bronstein, and to all the other teenage expats who spent so many hours teaching, explaining, discussing and adding information that I would never even have thought of, thank you—you have been a credit to your community and a blessing to me!

To the many expatriates who took the time to answer an impossible survey, challenge my statements, and provide me with insights, thank you all.

And finally to my husband John Craig of Otis Elevator Company, thank you for giving me a life of travel and adventure and the opportunity to live in Singapore.

How shall I go in peace and without sorrow? Nay, not without a wound in the spirit shall I leave this city.

(Kahlil Gibran, *The Prophet*)

JoAnn M. Craig
Singapore 1978

It's a sweltering and humid day. You've ordered a cold beer and it hasn't come yet! However, this type of behaviour will get you nowhere. If you really want good service, a quiet, respectful tone will do wonders. Note: In the East a pointing forefinger only adds insult to injury. *Photo: JoAnn Craig*

1 East vs West: Some Cultural and Personality Differences*

Temper Tantrums

A hot and sultry day; a misunderstanding at the bank; an inexperienced sales clerk; a "Sorry—no stock" answer; a bad day at the Registry of Vehicles: any of these may cause irritation or a flare of temper. In Western societies, anger can be expressed loudly and vociferously and usually no harm is done; often results are quick and forthcoming when one displays a show of righteous indignation. Here in the East, it is a different story. Speaking with a raised voice, shouting, swearing and violent displays of temper are considered inexcusable. The person involved will suffer a loss of face, and the person who has shown anger will suffer a loss of respect that he may never regain.

---

* By Western societies I am referring to the European nations as well as to the United States of America, Canada, Australia, New Zealand, etc., but for easier reading I will include them all under the heading "Western" rather than "Western-European".

Tone of Voice

Many Westerners speak in a loud and hearty voice, but among Eastern people, the more important the subject, the more quiet the voice! For some reason, many Westerners think that they can overcome a language barrier by speaking very LOUDLY. However, the problem is usually not one of deafness on the part of the listener, but simply one of language communication. Speaking s-l-o-w-l-y will be beneficial; hand signals or the aid of a pleasant passerby will also help in a situation like this. (The English have an instinctive understanding of the quiet, well-modulated tone, and this is enhanced by their more traditional reserve.)

Some Westerners (here the English seem to be the worst offenders) speak in monosyllables and a sort of clipped pidgin-style baby-talk to the locals. This is not necessary; Singaporeans are well-educated and they are often bi- or trilingual. Do not leave out articles and prepositions: "I go to shop ... be back . . . one hour." Speak in complete sentences.

Modesty and Reserve vs
Pride and Familiarity

Visitors from countries with a pioneering experience consider the traits of pride, boldness, aggressiveness, achievement, frankness and familiarity to be assets. While this may be true in some parts of the world (where they helped to carve a country out of the wilderness), it is just the opposite in the East. The virtues of humility, reserve, modesty and consensus are more greatly admired and respected. You may notice, especially in interactions with the Chinese community, that the people are modest in speech, and rarely boastful. Even in speaking about their children or possessions they will talk in a deprecating manner. The Western tendency to brag and boast about the feats of their children, for example, is not considered to be in good taste. Misunderstandings can occur when Westerners fail to understand this part of the Eastern psyche. To illustrate this, I'll quote the true story told to me by

Mr Wong of the Singapore China Society: "A rich merchant went to London and was entertaining some very important European guests. He had the affair catered at a famous hotel. In the Chinese manner, he said that he was sorry that the food and drink were not very fine. (This was intended to pay respect to the guests and it actually means that nothing is considered good enough for the honourable people who are being entertained. This is proper Chinese etiquette.) Some hotel employees overheard these remarks and the management, feeling quite insulted, proceeded to sue the merchant for defaming the character of the hotel." A more modest and more humble attitude on the part of the visitor to Singapore and Malaysia will improve his business and personal relationships—and aid his communication. Easy familiarity is a natural sign of friendliness to Americans and Australians and some others. A shock awaits the expat or tourist when he realizes that getting familiar is not thought of by the Asians as synonymous with getting friendly!

The "Back-home" Syndrome

The visitor can't help comparing the country he visits with his own home country. The cultural differences are striking. Remember to treat Singaporeans and Malaysians as you would like to be treated. They are justly proud of their countries and they resent statements like: "Back in the States we have bigger . . . better . . ." and "In France, our women are more . . ." and "In Italy, we . . .". A person can feel free to criticise his own family, friends or country, etc., but outsiders should never do it.

The Western Profile

Consider for a moment some traits that people have little control over: the average Westerner is giant-sized compared to the average Asian, he is very hairy, and he smells different (probably because of the vast amounts of meat that he consumes). Add to this picture what appears to be a loud and booming voice, an aggressive attitude, a clever, snappy answer to everything. Then compare this to the reserved attitude of the Asian. If we take a look at ourselves the way others might see us, we can tone ourselves down a bit so that we won't seem to be so overwhelming.

Sense of Humour

Eastern people sometimes seem to laugh out of context. They may laugh at situations that Westerners do not think are funny. However, the Easterner may not be laughing because he thinks that the situation is funny either. He often laughs when he feels shy, nervous or embarrassed. He laughs to hide a feeling of humiliation or "loss-of-face". For example, when the sales clerk drops the beautiful vase you have just bought, and there is not another one like it, she laughs because she feels embarrassed, not because she thinks it is funny. Or when the young nurse laughs at the strange shape of your son's broken arm, she does not laugh because she thinks it is funny, she laughs because she feels shy in the presence of such a good-looking young man!

Westerners should be aware of this difference in East-West reactions. If they understand why it happens, then they can cope with it and not feel angry or upset when they encounter it.

Compliments

Beware! Danger! Do not praise the Asian's beautiful child, do not pinch chubby cheeks, do not say how fat and healthy the child is looking, or how much the child has grown. Asians feel that compliments like these to a lovely child, a beautiful girl, a fat and dimpled baby will cause the "evil eye", i.e., some harm may come to the child or person who has been praised. Even today, some modern parents quickly take a bunch of chilli peppers and onions, burn them, and then draw an imaginary circle around the child's head three times with it; they then discard the peppers and onions. Sometimes salt is used in the purifying and counteracting action. Even if younger people scoff at this ritual, the parents still perform it, just in case! It is especially bad to give compliments in front of the children.

Note: Some Chinese call their children nicknames like "little dog" or "pig", etc. This fools the spirits into thinking that the children are not beautiful, fat and healthy. This ensures that the spirits will not become envious over the children, and harm them through jealousy.

First-name Basis

The Eastern etiquette follows the English style here of never calling an acquaintance by his first name unless asked to do so. Westerners often get down to business when meeting someone for the first time by calling him by his first name, often shortening it, or contracting it. They feel it shows friendliness and a lack of formality. In the Eastern culture it would be considered forward to do this. It is better to wait until the other person suggests that you call him by a more informal name.

Easterners usually address the parents or older members of a friend's family as "Aunty" or "Uncle", even if there is no relationship between them. In fact, the most polite thing one can do when one enters an Eastern home is to seek out the elder members before doing anything else, and greet them ("Hello Aunty" or "Hello Uncle"), just to announce your presence, and also to show them due respect.

Touching People

Westerners are a "touchy" people. They like to touch the people they are fond of. (Of course, this is not universal!) They feel it is polite to grab the elbow of their woman companion and guide her across the street—even though women are often capable of crossing streets on their own! They often pat, squeeze, or hug people. They kiss each other on greeting and departing. Eastern people are more reserved. When a man touches a woman, and vice versa, it is considered an unnatural form of intimacy. I first became aware of this when an

Keep your hands to yourself, Ms Expat! Touching across the sex line is taboo in Singapore and Malaysia. *Photo: JoAnn Craig*

expatriate wife called and asked if I would check up on an odd experience she had had in a shop. In trying to restrain a male clerk from taking down yards of silk material, she reached out and laid her hand on his arm. She had to make a hasty retreat from his appreciative glances! When I questioned Asians on their ethics, I learned that when a woman touches a man or vice versa, it is naturally taken as an amorous advance. They have restrictions attached to tactile relationships. This social taboo refers to touching people of the *opposite sex only*. Among the locals it is socially acceptable for men to walk with their arm on another man's shoulder, or for girls to hold hands. Westerners have mixed feelings about this. Americans and Australians usually don't mind touching people of the opposite sex, but they often feel an aversion to touching or holding hands with people of the same sex. Europeans may not be bothered by this as some European countries have similar customs.

Another experience was reported by an American girl. In her delight at meeting a Chinese friend whom she hadn't seen for a long time, she rushed up and gave him a hug. She immediately sensed that something was wrong when she felt him go stiff all over, and take a step backwards. Whenever she saw him after that, he immediately put his hands in front of him and assumed a pugilistic stance! So, when in Singapore or Malaysia, feel free to do your touching with the same sex, but keep a hands-off policy with members of the opposite sex.

Discussions on a Personal or Emotional Level

Westerners often speak on a deep and personal level. They strive for openness in their relationships with others. Because of this desire to reveal themselves to those they care about, they speak freely of their emotions, feelings, and personal experiences. This is acceptable and even desirable in many Western cultures. However, in the Asian culture, much value is placed on reserve. Even in a close relationship it would be embarrassing to discuss matters of a personal or intimate nature.

The open, direct and straightforward approach is seen as admirable to many Westerners. However, here in the East, if one opens oneself, it is thought to be a sign of weakness and or cowardliness. It is seen as humiliating to reveal your inner being. The one who "opens" is not to be trusted. He tells secrets!

Being of an inquisitive nature, I learned that it used to be common for Chinese men to have more than one wife. Today, this practice is not allowed in Singapore, but some of the older generation still have polygynous marriages. A Chinese friend told me that his father had two wives, and of course this brought a multitude of questions to my mind: Did he love both wives equally? How did he divide his time? Were the wives jealous? How did the half-brothers and half-sisters feel about each other? And so on and on! My poor friend was stunned. After a moment he said, "You should never ask Asians questions like these. They are things we don't discuss, not even with our parents." I seem to learn most of my lessons the hard way—I hope that it will be easier for you.

Conversely, very few Asians are aware of the Westerners' reluctance to discuss the price they paid for things, the amount of their salary, the rent on their apartment, etc. They don't realise that most money matters are "taboo" for Westerners in their conversations. When a Singaporean or a Malaysian asks you "How much did you pay?" he is merely expressing a friendly interest. When he says "Oh, too much, lah!" he is only trying to be helpful. Westerners should be aware that this is typical of local courtesy.

Offensive or Obscene Gestures
1   Pointing with the forefinger at a person is considered to be very bad manners. Use the thumb or the open hand when you need to point to someone.
2   Calling someone to you with a waving forefinger is uncouth in an Asian culture. It is like calling a dog. A beckoning gesture with the first two fingers of the hand is also in bad taste. The proper way to beckon to a person, taxi, etc. in Singapore and Malaysia is like this: use the whole hand, palm down, four fingers together, thumb folded across the palm or extended, and wave the hand with the palm facing inwards to your own body—rather as if you were shovelling money from a table into your left hand!
3   Making a fist and hitting it against the open palm of the opposite hand is an extremely rude gesture. It is analogous to the Spanish hand-signal, or the American freeway sign. It should never be done in mixed company. A dynamic Western executive closed a conference with his local staff using these words: ". . . and these are the

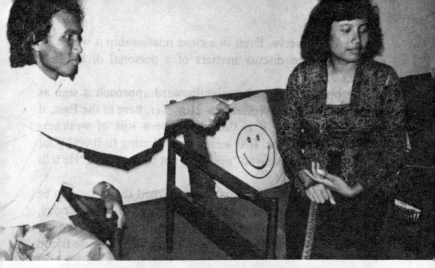

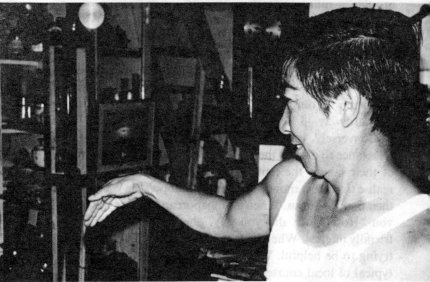

Top. It's good manners to point to a person with the thumb in this position. *Photo: JoAnn Craig*

Bottom. "Please come here" is gestured with the whole hand in a motion towards the body. Though Chinese, Malays and Indians all do it a bit differently, the principle is the same — the whole hand is involved, and sometimes the head makes a follow-through gesture. *Photo: JoAnn Craig*

objectives for the coming year." He punctuated this remark by loudly and distinctly slapping his fist against his palm. Of course, the meeting was broken up, the message was ambiguous, and the point was lost. He never knew what he had said or done to cause such a hilarious

Mr Ugly Expat strikes again! A gesture like this in mixed company can cause a startled reaction. *Photo: JoAnn Craig*

reaction. A comparable obscene gesture is making a fist with the thumb stuck between the first and second fingers.

4   You are at a party, or waiting for a taxi, and you have nothing to do with your hands. Wherever you put them, keep them off your hips—it is a sign of anger.

Ethnocentricity

What a lovely word—it's one of the biggest dangers in the anthropological world. Anthropologists are constantly on guard against it. It's one of the worst things a person can be accused of. What does it mean? A dictionary definition is: "Characterised by or based on the attitude that one's own group is superior." According to an anthropological definition, it means that one compares every other culture unfavourably with one's own culture; that one looks at other cultures through one's own eyes; that one reacts in a bigoted, prejudiced, or closed-minded way towards other cultures; that one sees one's own culture as virtuous or select and feels that one's own standard of values is universally and intrinsically true—and that one views one's own customs as the original human ones, and views all other customs as somehow inferior. It is seen in the "Back home, we do it this way" attitude. It creeps in when it is least expected, and it sometimes happens to the best of people. Often unconscious, it can occur even when one is determined to appreciate everything about the foreign culture one is visiting or living in.

An example of this can be seen during the "durian" season in Singapore and Malaysia. This season is characterised by the local people frantically dragging home huge sacks of this peculiar-smelling fruit. The odour lingers for hours in elevators and stairwells. Physiologically speaking, human noses work in the same manner. But, culturally speaking, they are very different. Why durian smells like heaven to some people and like garlic-flavoured custard to others is a matter of ethnocentricity. To understand and appreciate another culture, one must have an open mind, and, if possible, an open nose!

Buying a durian takes some expertise. It must have the right smell and the right "sound" which is obtained by shaking the fruit. When a Westerner admits to loving durians, he is considered an honorary Asian! *Photo: Times Publishing, Singapore*

Asian "Yes"

When Asians say "yes", they sometimes mean "I hear what you are saying, but I do not necessarily agree!" An Asian "yes" may mean "no" or "maybe". Many Westerners mistake this as a sign of not being trustworthy. However, many Asians still follow the Eastern ethic of not questioning or disagreeing with a superior. To say an untruth is not considered as bad as making the other person "lose face", or hurting his feelings, or making him unhappy.

One Asian explains it like this: "When I don't want to make you feel bad, I say 'yes' with my mouth, but 'no' with my face or my actions." Some Asians almost never use the word "no".

Formality

Asian cultures are much more formal and traditional than Western cultures. Asians appreciate and respect preliminaries and form. Westerners often make decisions in an atmosphere of informality, giving little time for preliminaries.

The Easterners often measure the importance of a deal by how much formality surrounds it, and how many preliminaries lead up to it. Westerners often want to get straight to the heart of the matter, feeling that formality wastes time and money.

In Singapore, this may not be true so much as the Singaporeans have been dealing with Westerners for quite some time in their policy of industrialization. They are getting quite used to Western ways of business. In some parts of Malaysia, this formality may be more noticeable.

Asian "Face"

In investigating this phenomenon, I questioned a young Singaporean student who was attending university in Australia. I asked him to tell me about the biggest culture "shock" he had experienced when he went to live in Australia. He said: "You know, the biggest thing that I noticed was that people don't worry about 'face'! If you go to a party in Australia, you are expected to bring along your own bottle of spirits. Here, the Asian host would feel insulted (he would lose face) if someone did that. It might imply that his guest did not think that he could provide enough for him to drink!"

Loss of face is a difficult concept to understand. It has been described as: making someone feel embarrassed; making someone feel humiliated; causing someone to feel inferior; giving insult to someone.

Loss of face is most noticeable in dealings between superiors and subordinates. For instance, an Asian child or teenager (adult Asians as well!) would never disagree publicly with his parents. He would never want them to lose face. An Asian, especially in an extended family, would cause loss of face to his brothers, sisters, mother, father, etc., if he behaved in any way so as to cause them embarassment. A family, even though poor, is obliged to have a large wedding feast, for example, and invite all the family, friends, and relatives. If this is not done, the family would suffer loss of face. If a subordinate argues or disagrees with a superior in a business organization, the superior would suffer loss of face. If a student questions a teacher, the teacher would suffer loss of face. This can help to explain why an Asian employee may publicly agree with his Western employer while he privately continues to do things his own way. A Westerner feels this type of behaviour is dishonest, while an Asian feels this behaviour is polite.

For the Westerner

In spite of the hints that are given to many expats on understanding the Eastern psyche, many a Westerner still feels that the safest policy is to "be yourself: your open—friendly— and outspoken—self!" These qualities are supposed to be what other people admire most about Westerners. However, because of hundreds of years of cultural conditioning, whether it be in "loss of face" or in crowded living conditions, the Asian is less likely to admire the Westerner for his friendliness, outspokenness, and frankness, than he is to view him as lacking grace, manners and cleverness. Many times, what the Westerner feels is normal in his culture, is seen as irritating to people of other cultures.

Note: I don't wish to give the impression that Westerners must restrain their warm and friendly feelings towards their Asians hosts—quite the contrary. I would wish to encourage them to have better cross-cultural relations. I am only pointing out that misunderstandings can occur when people's assumptions have failed to be met on both sides. Asians are willing to overlook many things and forgive all kinds of mistakes when they know that the visitor's heart is in the right place. The fact that people care means more than outward conformity to custom.

2 Some Common Courtesies and Customs

Driving

1   The local people generally watch the front end of their automobile, and feel that the rear will take care of itself!

2   Buses often assume the right of way. They do have total right of way in the bus lanes during certain peak hours. In Singapore, on weekdays, these are between 0730 and 0930 hours and between 1630 and 1900 hours; on Saturday, between 0730 and 0930 hours and between 1130 and 1400 hours. In Malaysia, bus lanes are in operation only in Kuala Lumpur at the moment. The hours of operation are between 0715 and 0900 hours and between 1600 and 1830 hours on weekdays. There are no bus lane restrictions on Sundays and public holidays in both Singapore and Malaysia. Others must not use these lanes at all during these hours. (Maximum fine, $50 in Singapore, $500 in Malaysia.)

3   A hand stretched from the driver's side (either front or back seat) does not necessarily mean that a lady is drying

her nail varnish or a gentleman is indicating the place where he has had his last accident. It generally signifies that the car will be turning right or moving into the right lane. A hand waving in counter-clockwise circles, also from the driver's side, means that the car will be turning left shortly, or moving into the left lane. Any passenger in the car may take it upon himself to help the driver out with hand signals, even though their signals may be wrong and confuse other drivers.

4   In Singapore, do not drive into restricted zones (called the Central Business District or just CBD) between 0730 and 1015 hours on weekdays and Saturdays (excluding Sundays and public holidays), unless you have 4 persons in the car. Maximum fine $50!

5   If a car breaks down, the local people put a branch in the bumper or rear mudguard, or they lift the hood. These are visible signs that the car is not working and that the traffic must go around it. If possible, the car should be pushed to the left side of the road so as to cause as little obstruction as possible to the flow of traffic.

No, this car has not sprouted a tree — it is only out of order.
Photo: JoAnn Craig

6　An accident must be reported within twenty-four hours to the police, even if there is no injury or major damage.

7　Singaporean and Malaysian drivers are generally aggressive. (They have been known to assume Jekyll-Hyde personalities behind the wheel!) Defensive driving is recommended. However, there is a courtesy-in-driving campaign on in Singapore and Malaysia and rude or inconsiderate drivers are being fined. Be warned!

Elevators
The one nearest the door gets on and off first, man or woman. If you are planning on getting off in just a few stops, try to get on the elevator last. Do not smoke in an elevator. (Maximum fine $500 in Singapore.)

Fridays and Shopping in Malaysia
The following states in Malaysia observe Friday as a public holiday: Kedah, Perlis, Kelantan, Trengganu. In Perak, Selangor, Negri Sembilan, Pahang, Penang and Malacca, Sunday is a public holiday. Offices give time off for Muslim employees to go to the mosque on Fridays. Shops are normally closed on Friday in Kedah, Perlis, Kelantan and Trengganu. Places of entertainment like the cinema are also closed on this day.

Jay-walking
There is a campaign on in Singapore and Malaysia to discourage jay-walking. Cross only at approved places: overhead bridges, zebra crossings (indicated by pedestrian signs) and traffic lights. Maximum fine for jay-walking is $50 in Singapore, $25 in Malaysia. There is also a fine for motorists who do not give way to pedestrians crossing at approved places and times. (These fines may be increased in the future.)

Plants
Singapore and Malaysia have an anti-mosquito campaign. They are trying to eradicate disease-carrying mosquitos. If

you use saucers or drip-dishes under your potted plants, empty them often, for mosquitos breed in stagnant water. You may be fined if you disregard this law.

Official Parties, Business Lunches and Dinners

1 *Official parties:* Printed invitations to official parties must be acknowledged with a written acceptance or refusal. Wives, relatives or friends should not attend unless it is specifically stated on the invitation.

2 *Business lunches and dinners:* When inviting a guest for lunch or dinner, be specific. Ask for a definite date and suggest a time and a place. Don't say "Let's have lunch" as this assumes that each will pay his own way. Note: Men expect to pay for a woman's meal in Singapore and Malaysia. They are startled if a woman tries to pay for them.

3 Don't discuss business until after you have ordered a drink or cocktail and given your order to the waiter.

4 If your guest is a man, he gives his order directly to the waiter (unless it is a Chinese meal where the host assumes the responsibility for planning the courses). If the guest is a woman, she gives her order to the gentleman.

5 Business should not be discussed if wives are included in the dinner party.

Private Parties — Tips for the Hostess and the Guests

Private dinner parties in Singapore and Malaysia are a mixture of Eastern and Western customs and courtesies. Common sense and good manners are usually all that are required, but there are a few customs that the Westerner should be aware of:

1 Asian children wait for older persons to begin eating before they dig in themselves. They often invite the elders, personally, to have a hearty appetite and to start the meal.

2 At a dinner party, the host and hostess usually sit opposite each other, with the guests sitting in between. Often, the

wife of the host sits next to the wife of the guest, contrary to the Western practice of placing a man and a woman (who are not married to each other) next to one another.

3   In an Asian home, it is not polite for guests to go directly to the bathroom without first asking the hostess if they can use it.

4   The Asian hostess often invites the ladies to use the bathroom after dinner. She usually brings them there and waits for them until the last lady has finished.

Restaurants

1   Dress in most restaurants is casual. Some hotels and top-bracket restaurants require a jacket and tie. It is a good idea to check on this when making reservations. Women dress smartly for top-bracket restaurants and clubs. It's wise to bring a light shawl or sweater as the air-conditioning can make some places quite chilly.

2   The woman follows the captain to the dining table; if he does not pull the chair out for her, then the gentleman should seat her.

3   To summon a waiter, catch his eye, using the "beckoning gesture" (see page 9). Do not hiss, snap your fingers or shout "Waiter", "Boy", "*Garcon*", etc.

Shopping

A tourist should always be wary of "touts". These are people who sidle up to you and tell you that they can take you to a special shop where they can get you a good discount. You'll do much better if you browse and compare prices yourself.

Westerners are often confused by the methods of shopping and bargaining in Singapore and Malaysia. There are no hard and fast rules, but there are generalities that can be applied:

1   In large shopping centres, department stores or food markets, the prices are fixed—no bargaining is expected.

2   In the smaller shops, the shopkeepers will often offer a discount to customers, but bargaining is also recommended. A careful shopper will compare prices in several

shops before committing himself to an expensive purchase. Prices can vary considerably in shops that are just a block or so apart.

3   At the *pasar malam* (night market) and stall-type shops (in Arab Street, Thieves' Market, Change Alley, etc. in Singapore, or Petaling Street, Jalan Chow Kit, Jalan Tuanku Abdul Rahman, etc., in Kuala Lumpur) bargaining is essential. If a Westerner buys any merchandise without bargaining, he would be thought of as *bodoh* (stupid). The local people normally bargain before they pay for any goods; as a result, they may only pay about 40-50 per cent of the quoted price. The haggling should start somewhere around 30-40 per cent of the quoted price. The stall-keeper may reduce the price to 70-80 per cent. The customer should counter with about 50 per cent of the price, and, if it does not appear to be successful, he should begin to walk away. The stall-keeper in most instances would call the shopper back and settle for a lower price which could be around 50-60 per cent of the original price, or at any rate much lower than the originally quoted price.

4   Bargaining is usually distasteful to the Westerner; it has rarely been a part of his cultural background. However, in many parts of the East it is an expected part of the process and without it a very important element in the marketing structure is lost. If a person can get the hang of it, a warm feeling will be generated between the buyer and seller and a general sense of satisfaction and pleasure can be gained on both sides.

5   Be good-humoured and make up as many outrageous reasons for paying a lower price as you can; the entertainment you thereby provide will often work to your profit.

6   Do not allow yourself to be "psyched" by a shopkeeper. Many of those dealing with tourists can play a deft hand at amateur psychology. Because you are given a bottle of coke or a cold beer and encouraged to talk about your holiday, family, home, etc., it does not mean that you are

"But that's an unlucky number — if you charge me that I'll walk out of here and break my leg. What's your best price?" Good-humoured bargaining adds to the fun of shopping, and often to your benefit. This expat seems to have got the hang of bargaining, but she is not aware of the forbidden finger! *Photo: JoAnn Craig*

obligated to buy an article at a price which you feel is too high. If you find a shopkeeper who is more than fair with you, keep him in mind for future purchases. When you do your comparison shopping, he will most likely give you a better price than the other shops if you tell him the lowest price you were offered.

Smoking and Littering

1   Smoking is not allowed in cinemas, theatres, elevators and public transportation in Singapore. It is also not allowed in cinemas in all major towns in Malaysia. (Maximum fine $500!) One should ask for permission before smoking in a private home.

2   Do not throw butts, cigarette wrappers, bus tickets, etc. on the streets or sidewalks. There are receptacles for refuse near bus-stops and along the streets. This is not just a matter of good etiquette—there is a $500 maximum fine for littering.

Taxis

1   Every taxi in Singapore must have a working meter. The driver should set the flag as soon as the taxi starts to move. Some taxis in Malaysia do not have meters; in these cases, the price should be fixed before starting the journey. Before engaging a taxi, it is a good idea to ask a passerby to give you an idea of the approximate price you should pay to reach your destination.

2   There is no bargaining on rates.

3   There is an extra charge for baggage, whether carried in front or in the boot (trunk).

4   There is an extra charge for more than two passengers. Look for the list of surcharges usually fixed on the inside back door of taxis.

5   If you have left something in the taxi, call the Registry of Vehicles (R.O.V.) in Singapore or the Registrar and Inspector of Motor Vehicles (R.I.M.V.) in Malaysia. Drivers are very good about turning in lost merchandise.

6   When an empty taxi passes you by, and the driver makes a waggling motion with his hand, it means that he is on his way to change shift, or else he is hurrying to "take his *makan*" (eat a meal).

7   If by some unfortunate chance you should have a problem with a taxi driver, take down his number. You can report him to the R.O.V. in Singapore or the R.I.M.V. in

Malaysia. The authorities are very concerned that tourists are treated fairly. They will deal with any complaint that you make.

Tipping

Tipping is an individual matter. Customs vary here. The local people generally do not tip taxi-drivers, doormen, hair-dressers,etc. During the Chinese New Year festival, they may give a *hong bao* (red packet containing money) to someone who does them a special service.

1   *General:* Do not tip when there is a sign displayed that says "No Tipping". Airport employees and employees of private clubs are not tipped. Government employees, meter readers, office clerks, etc. should never be tipped. To offer to do so could cause them embarrassment and/or trouble.

2   *Hotels:* Tourists generally tip in hotels. It is a personal decision. They should not tip a doorman unless he calls a taxi for them or provides some other service. Room and messenger service requires a tip of from 50 cents to $2. Hotels ordinarily add a service charge to the bill.

3   *Restaurants:* Most restaurants add a 10 per cent service charge. You may leave more if you wish. If no surcharge has been added, then a tip of 10 to 15 per cent of the bill is fair. The head waiter is not tipped unless he provides a special service, such as reserving a choice table—then folding money, not coins, should be used.

4   *Taxis:* Tourists often tip taxi-drivers, but it is not necessary. A tip of 20 to 40 cents is normal if you prefer to do so.

Toilet Facilities

1   In hotels and the larger department stores, western toilet facilities are usually available. In smaller shops and local bathrooms, there may be the typical "squat type" of toilet (more about this later). No special instructions are needed for their use. Just don't be surprised to see them.

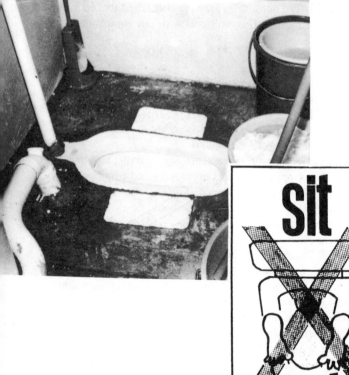

Top. A typical squat toilet.

Right. This sign is displayed in the toilets of an enterprising local department store. Expats have asked that the store make this sign available for sale! *Photo: courtesy of Mr Loo, C.K. Tang Department Store*

2   *Toilets in local homes:* (This is a delicate subject. I hope
    that it does not cause embarrassment.) You may wonder
    what the bucket of water and bailing scoop are doing in
    the local's bathroom, or what the extra tap is for. This is
    because:
    (a) most locals prefer a splash-bath to a shower and use
         the scoop to pour water over themselves.
    (b) Malays and Indians, and even some others, insist on
         washing themselves every time they defecate; the
         left hand is used for this purpose. They feel that just
         wiping with paper is unclean. (Indeed they may be
         right!) If you have local guests, it is well to be aware
         of this and provide the necessary water and bailing
         scoop.

There are some locals who are not used to toilet seats and
prefer squatting over the typical flush-floor local toilet. There
is some medical evidence, I believe, that this is a more
natural and healthier position in any case. But it can lead to
awkward situations with the unsophisticated local—standing
or squatting on your toilet seat, and maybe missing, for
instance! Some local men who are not used to Western-type
toilets may not realise that the toilet seat should be raised
before urinating. One has several options here:

1   Inform male guests of the practice of raising the toilet
    seat.
2   Leave it raised—and hope that it will be left that way.
3   Keep quiet about it, and clean the toilet seat before using
    it yourself.

ASIAN ETIQUETTE
Pertaining to the Chinese,
Malay and Indian Sections

Singapore and Malaysia are rapidly modernizing and industrializing. Some of the younger or "more modern" folks are adopting "Western Ways". Some of them, unfortunately, are losing touch with their own customs and culture. The habits and courtesies on the following pages may be considered "old fashioned" or "out-of-date" by some Westernized Asians; however, the Western guest in Singapore or Malaysia is advised to learn them and to understand them, as they are the everyday patterns of behaviour for the majority of the local people.

An appreciation of and an acceptance of Asian cultural behaviour will help to ease the pain of culture shock (impact) for the expatriate, the tourist and the visitor to these countries. It will also help to develop the traits necessary for a successful cultural adjustment for expatriates, i.e., cultural empathy, tolerance, and a sense of cultural relativity.

An understanding of the differences between Eastern and Western cultures can help to build a bridge of friendship and cooperation between us.

3 The Chinese Community

THE PEOPLE

This book will not deal with the history, religion and festivals of the Chinese community in Singapore and Malaysia. There is a lot of published information on these topics and I suggest that you visit a good bookstore and purchase some material that will help you to appreciate the unique features of this culture. To help you gain an insight into the Chinese psyche, I will be adding some background material from time to time.

In Singapore and Malaysia, there are some wonderful guides who can take you on a walking tour of the local Chinatown. They can show you the shops where Panama hats, wooden clogs and sandlewood statues are still skillfully handcrafted. They can take you to a dimly-lit Taoist temple where a spiritualist medium will go into a trance and write out magic papers to protect you from harm. They can tell you marvellous stories about why Chinese cats have no tails. (It seems that if you cut off the tail of a cat, this prevents it from jumping over the body of a dead person. If the cat has a

A *Sam Sui* woman. These women are rarely seen today, and very difficult to photograph. They adhere to the old superstition that a part of their soul can be captured by a camera if they are photographed.
Photo: Times Publishing, Singapore

tail, it can jump over a dead body and the dead person will then become a zombie. The only way to stop a zombie from harming anyone is to hit him with the handle of a broom. Of course, you will have to hear the whole story from the guide in order to appreciate it thoroughly.)

While in Singapore or Malaysia, try and see if you can spot a "Black and White" *amah* (housekeeper and child-tender). She will be wearing a spotlessly clean white blouse and a pair of black cotton or silk trousers. She may have a long pig-tail hanging down her back (a symbol of her eternal and voluntary spinsterhood). She is a highly valued domestic servant in European families. She is reliable and untiring in her service.

Also, look for a *Sam Sui* woman. You can find her around construction sites as she is a building labourer. She will be wearing a royal blue *samfoo* (Chinese trouser-suit) and on her head will be a bright red stiffly-starched hat. She will have a marvellous face, deeply tanned and etched with lines from spending long hours working under the hot sun every day. These women will usually have a very beautiful piece of jade, a bracelet, etc., which they believe will break before any of their bones will. They feel that the jade will absorb the shock of any accident and protect them from physical harm. These women are especially noted for their safe work habits. Employers prefer to hire them as they are rarely late or absent.

The Black and White *amahs* and the *Sam Sui* women were early forerunners of the Women's Liberation Movement. Many years ago they broke away from China in a rebellion against marriage and took vows of spinsterhood. (Today, some do marry, but then the husband has to stay at home and do the housework!) In China, marriage was often a depressing condition in the old days. A daughter-in-law was the "lowest man on the totem pole" in her husband's house. She had few rights. These brave women rebelled in a fight for individual freedom in a highly conservative and traditional society. They left their homes, and travelled to a new and strange land to better their condition at a time when women's rights were

Taking photos in a temple is usually permitted, but it is polite to ask for permission first. With three bows and lighted joss-sticks these ladies greet the gods and pay respects to their ancestors. The three bows are to Heaven, Earth and Mankind (the Universe). *Photo: Straits Times, Singapore*

Two retired Black and White *amahs* of today relax in the serenity of their *gongxi* garden. These women are taking a well-deserved rest; there is time now for peace, prayers and companionship. There is no fear for the future for their *gongxi* cares for them in sickness and in health, and even in death. *Photo: Joe Craig*

Two Black and White *amahs* of yesterday. These lovely young women have tied up their hair and renounced prospects of marriage and motherhood, choosing to live a respected life of hard work and independence. *Photo courtesy of Mr Keng Ah Wong*

unheard of. They formed a sisterhood to protect themselves and to give mutual care and support to each other. Their life resembled a religious community (and still does today). Most of them are vegetarians and they spend their free time in common association and in prayer. They live together in *gongxi* (a colloquial term which means "public company" or "trading company"; in Singapore and Malaysia it is used to denote a group of single persons who live together and share household expenses and duties). Many of them have gone through a ceremony of "tying up the hair". It resembles a marriage ceremony but the result is to "conclude affinity". This means that they have given up all ideas of getting married. A celebration is held, and the girl's friends and family bring *hong bao** and presents. Her hair is ceremoniously "put up" to symbolize that she is now considered "as if married" and she can never be given in marriage to anyone. Three days later, she lets her hair down into a pigtail again, and enters the society with respect.

These women are tough, hardy and self-sufficient. Their *gongxi* provides them with a home when they are not working, and becomes an old-age retirement centre for them when they are finished with work. The women take care of each other during illness and bury each other when they die. These women work well into their old age, right into their seventies and eighties, in some cases. A *Sam Sui* woman can carry a 100-pound sack of cement on her back as easily as a baby. A Black and White *amah* will often be called back from retirement, as women of her kind are a rarity in today's modern times. Young girls do not choose this life anymore, and when these brave women are gone, there will be no one to replace them.

There is a curious phenomenon in the Catholic "Novena" Church of St. Alphonsus in Singapore. Pious old Chinese

---

* A small red gift packet that is used to contain money. The money is given in even numbers and an even amount.

Buddhists bring offerings of flowers and mix freely with young Christian students singing modern hymns. Buddhists, Taoists, Confucianists and Hindus pray alongside Catholics and Christians. The object of their devotion is the Virgin Mary. People from every faith flock to this church to pray for her intercession. The Chinese consider her to be a representation of Kwan Yin, the Goddess of Mercy. The Redemptorists, who are in charge of this church, feel that the power of prayer and the ecumenical spirit that prevails transcends the separation of the different faiths. Most Catholic churches in Kuala Lumpur conduct these "Novena" services on Saturday. The Redemptorists in Ipoh have services along the same lines.

Seventy-six per cent of the people of Singapore and thirty-five per cent of the people of Malaysia are Chinese.

LEARNING TO SOCIALIZE

Introductions
1   Shaking hands between people of the different sexes is acceptable among the Chinese. (Note: This is not true for the Indians and Malays.) The woman takes the lead here. If she wishes to shake hands with a man, she offers her hand first. If she doesn't, then a man should not offer his.
2   The Western practice of *saying the name* of the most important person first is good etiquette; the most important person is:
    (a)   the higher-ranking before the lower-ranking: "Mr Vice-President, this is my assistant, Mr Tan."
    (b)   the older person before the younger: "Mr Wong, this is my nephew, Mr Jones."
    (c)   the woman before the man: "Miss Lim, this is Mr Wong."

Greetings
1   In business, the polite Chinese will say, "Is your business prosperous?" The response will be, "My business is moderate."

2   Socially, the Chinese greet each other with "Have you eaten your fill?" or "Have you taken your food?" The response is "Yes, thank you" (even if you are starving)! This exchange of greetings is analogous to the Western "How are you?" "Fine, thank you."

3   Chinese men often greet each other with a friendly pat on the arm. A Western greeting is acceptable among the modern Chinese of Singapore and Malaysia. Do not hug or kiss Chinese friends unless you have a "close" relationship.

Names

1   Contrary to the Western manner of having a Christian name first, a middle name second and the surname third, the Chinese (if they are not using a Westernized name) put their surname first, their middle name next and their proper name last. For example:

Chinese			*Western*		
TAN	HOCK	SENG	JOHN	DAVID	JONES
(surname)	(middle name)	(proper name)	(proper name)	(middle name)	(surname)

2   Chinese trace their descent through the male line. Traditionally, only the father's relations were considered important as a woman gave up membership in her own family on marriage. Today, modern Chinese maintain close ties with their mother's relations as well.

3   An explanation of Chinese names: In the example given above, *Tan* is the surname of the individual. He should be called Mr Tan. *Hock* is the name usually given to all the sons in the family. For instance, Tan Hock Seng's brother may be called Tan Hock Chye. (In some Chinese families, however, the third name is the common one for all the sons and the middle name is the one the individual is called by, as in Lim Seng Yew and Lim Beng Yew.)

4   It is a good idea to ask how the person prefers being called if the relationship is on a more personal level. Sometimes

an individual will use the third name alone: Seng, in the example given. At other times he may prefer to be called Hock Seng. Sometimes he will use a Westernized name like Danny Tan. He may even prefer to be called by his initials, "H.S.", or by a nickname or a shortened form of his name. Note: many Chinese, especially Christians and those who have attended English-medium schools, have Western names.

5   In the Chinese style, women do not change their surnames on marriage. They retain their patrilineal name (their father's surname). A Westerner can refer to Tan Hock Seng's wife as Mrs Tan but her friends call her Lee Poh Choo, or simply Poh Choo.

SOME COMMON COURTESIES AND CUSTOMS

Temples

1   The right door is used for entry and the left door for exit (as in the Chinese operas). The polite visitor will follow this custom.
2   It is not necessary to remove the shoes, but it is a good idea for men to remove their hats.
3   Taking photographs is usually permitted, but it is a good idea to ask for permission first.

Shopping

1   It is bad luck to *ask* for a debt early in the morning. You should wait until after 1100 hours at least. It is good luck to *pay* a debt early in the morning, it is a sign of good fortune for the rest of the day.
2   The local shopkeeper feels that it is a bad sign if the *first* customer of the day leaves without making a purchase. He will make a special effort to obtain a sale from his first customer, i.e. offer a discount, give a special price, etc. If you are only window shopping it would be better to

wait until later on in the day. If you find yourself inadvertently being a first customer, please buy something small so you won't ruin the whole day for him! A pack of matches or a greeting card will do.

If the customer refuses to buy something, some of the older Chinese may fill a pail with water and toss it out onto the street to wash away the bad luck. The water is not aimed at the customer. It will be as if the impolite customer had never come by.

Favours
When the Chinese ask a favour of an important man, i.e., a letter of introduction, a business recommendation, etc., they usually accompany the request with two bottles of brandy tied together with a red ribbon, and some fruit.

Invitations
When sending invitations to Chinese friends, use red or pink paper (a sign of joy). White and blue are sad colours, used in funerals. It is permissible to use a white card if the printing is in red, pink or gold lettering though.

Visiting a Chinese Home
1   The Chinese do not have religious restrictions about wearing shoes in the home, but many of them will have beautiful marble or polished wooden floors. They feel it is inconsiderate to wear shoes that may mar or soil them. Even if the floors are not beautiful, they would not like dust being tracked in!

It is a good idea to quickly glance around to see if members of the family have removed their shoes, then follow suit. If you ask if you should remove your shoes, the polite answer may be "No", but you might be considered uncouth if you don't take them off anyway. They sometimes protest if you remove them, but you will still be thought of as having been raised properly.

2   It is proper to bring a gift of fruit, sweets or cakes on the third or fourth visit. If you bring something on the first visit it will give the impression that you are trying to bribe your way to a friendship. So establish a friendship before giving gifts. It is appropriate to say that the sweets are "for the children". This is done to show that the giver does not assume that the receiver is greedy. The happy receiver can accept the gift without loss of face, and then feel free to eat up all the sweets himself. Always bring an even number: this is a sign of happiness and good luck. Bring four or eight oranges, two bags of sweets, etc. The host may return some of your gift, i.e. if you bring some oranges, he may give two of them back to you as you leave. This is to return some of the good luck.

3   The Chinese entertain guests in their living room. They will not show visitors through the house, especially the bedrooms. Even family members do not enter each other's rooms without permission. They think it is quite funny when a Westerner shows them the whole house (from the attic to the cellar, and even the closets)!

On Being a House Guest

1   In the morning, a knock on the door will be a summons for breakfast. It is polite for the guest to "join the family" for meals. The guest should wait until the entire family is seated before taking the seat that will be provided for him. (The same rule applies for lunch and dinner.) The host will seat him.

2   The Chinese family never wastes any food. It is common to leave unfinished food on the serving plates after meals. The next morning, all the food that has been left over will be cooked up with some vegetables and served for breakfast or lunch. This is the origin of "Chop Suey".

3   The female guest will never wash underwear, etc., in a wash basin while staying with a Chinese family. Be sure to bring enough clean clothes to last throughout your visit.

In an emergency, ask your hostess for advice about doing your laundry. The reason for this is that it would be an insult to the host to see unmentionables hanging up to dry. Only a wild and wanton woman would tempt a man with this display!

4   Guests should never wander about the house without a member of the family. This goes back to the old days when many Chinese buried their treasure in large jars under the floor boards. If a guest went walking around, the family might think that he was feeling with his feet for the loose board that covered the family jewels.

5   Chinese are very hospitable. They may never tell you if you are committing a *faux pas*. If you see a funny expression on the face of your host—an upturned eye movement and a slight twist of the neck—try to find out what you are doing wrong. You might ask a younger member of the family for advice.

Gifts

1   "Oh no, you shouldn't . . . no need", etc. The Chinese will accept a gift with disclaimers. This is the polite form for the recipient to follow. The giver should not be taken aback by this and think that this gift is not appreciated. The giver need only say "I'm pleased that you accept it."

2   The Chinese consider it bad manners to open a gift in front of the giver. Don't be offended if it is set aside until after you have left.

3   "Bread-and-butter" gifts: A thank-you note and a gift of food will always be appreciated by the Chinese. Some nice gifts to give are:

   (a)   a food hamper (a large basket of grocery delicacies, available from most supermarkets)

   (b)   some fine cakes in reusable tins (the tins make good baking pans)

   (c)   a lovely box of chocolates and a tin of cookies or biscuits. (Remember to give in pairs).

4   Some things carry an element of bad luck or can be taken as an ill omen. The following should be avoided when buying gifts:

(a) *Straw sandals:* They are worn at funerals. A Chinese would have to make many offerings to the ancestors to avoid the bad luck associated with a present like this.

(b) *A stork on baby-shower paper, or in a floral arrangement:* In some Western cultures, the stork is associated with the arrival of a baby. The classic answer to the question: "Mommy, where did I come from?" is "The stork brought you, of course!" In the Hokkien culture the long-legged heron (which looks just like a stork) is a symbol of a woman's death. It is carried on top of a hearse to show that a woman has died. An unfortunate misunderstanding occurred when a young Chinese mother was presented with a lovely floral arrangement that had a stork nestled on top of it. There were two bad omens here: (1) the flowers, which are only given to the sick (and new mothers are not thought of as being sick), and (2) the stork, which resembles a symbol of a woman's death.

    Even though the Chinese mother was young and Westernized, the double-death omen was too much for her. The American friend, who had gone to a lot of trouble to find the stork, never knew that the new mother was in tears when her husband arrived later on that evening.

(c) *Clocks:* The Cantonese word for "clock" can also mean "to go to a funeral", so a clock as a gift can be taken as a bad omen.

(d) *White, blue or black gifts:* These colours are associated with funerals. Red, pink and yellow are joyful colours. Many young Singaporeans may not be concerned about the colour of a gift, but, to be on the safe side, stick with the happy colours.

(e) *Sharp objects, knives, scissors:* These symbolize the cutting off of a friendship.

(f) *Flowers:* Since the Chinese love food, and flowers cannot be eaten, they usually don't give them to each other as presents.

    (i) Flowers can be sent to people who are sick in hospital. They can also be sent to funerals.

    (ii) A young gentleman does not bring or send flowers to a lady: that would be treating her as if she were sick.

    (iii) It is the custom of many Westerners to send flowers to a hostess after a dinner party. In Singapore or Malaysia, it would be better to send candy or a basket of fruit instead.

    (iv) The French and German custom of giving an uneven number of flowers as a gift, e.g., five roses, would be a double disaster. (Bad omens: flowers and uneven number.)

(g) *Handkerchiefs:* The Chinese consider these a sign of sadness. They feel that they will cause grief or break off a friendship. Handkerchiefs are often given to mourners at a funeral.

5   To the Chinese, happiness is "born a twin", hence all gifts should come in pairs. This signifies the joy of being a couple. Single items and odd numbers are a sign of separation, loneliness and death.

FOOD AND DRINK

Eating and drinking are the favourite pastimes of the Chinese. Dining is an art, polished to fine perfection! They believe that eating is not only good for the body, but that it is also good for the spirit! This is probably why no decent Chinese would visit a friend at mealtimes without a gift of food, why no Chinese would greet a friend without inquiring as to whether or not he has eaten, why if a Chinese wishes to break off a meeting, he makes subtle hints about not having eaten yet.

The Chinese have discovered a way to prepare and make tasty every edible object on earth. There is a Chinese saying that anything which walks with its back to the sky can be eaten! They use food for curing illnesses, to celebrate an event (any event!) and to honour their friends. The Chinese love to talk about food. Being great diplomats, they feel that it is foolish to discuss religion, sex and politics. (Westerners often feel the same!)

Here are some other Chinese dining generalities:

1 In a Chinese meal, the more festive the occasion, the more courses will be served. The Western custom of serving three-course meals may be taken as a sign that the occasion is not an important one. Most Chinese are aware of the Western practice of three-course meals; they would only be offended if they were invited to a *Chinese* meal that consisted of three courses.

2 Many Chinese (Buddhists) do not eat beef. When serving dinner to Chinese friends, it is safer to serve chicken, fish or pork.

3 In the Western culture, the white meat of the chicken is considered to be the choicest part. In the East, the opposite is true. The red or dark portions are the most desirable. When serving chicken, it is polite to offer the dark parts (wings and thighs especially) to the Chinese guests. A wonderful old Chinese gentleman had been served chicken breasts at an official Western dinner party. It wasn't until we began discussing dining etiquette that he realised he had not been slighted by the offering of the white parts.

4 The Chinese dislike mutton: "too smelly", "too heaty". ("Heaty" is a term difficult to explain, for even Chinese friends differ in their interpretations. Some say that "heaty" foods make the body feel too hot, too full and too uncomfortable. Certain illnesses are caused by eating too

much "heaty" food, e.g. a sore throat. Chocolate, granola and most meats are examples of "heaty" foods. "Cooling" foods are the opposite of "heaty" foods. They can also cause or aggravate an illness, e.g. a cold or a cough, and they are not supposed to be taken on cool days. Tea, yoghurt and water-melon are examples of "cooling" foods. I can't give an exhaustive list of "heaty" and "cooling" foods here, but draw any Chinese into conversation about food and he will be only too glad to advise you.)

5 Some Chinese do not like milk, yoghurt, etc. It seems to upset their stomachs.

6 The Chinese prefer their fish, prawns, etc. with the heads, tails and skin left on. These parts are often considered the best delicacies!

7 At a dinner party, the men would be pleased with straight brandy and beer served *with* their meals, not after! They enjoy a good Chinese wine, but are not too familiar with Western wines. As a rule, they do not enjoy water and coffee with dinner. They also drink fine brandy with 7-up, ginger-ale, etc.

8 Many local people salt their fruit and put ice in their beer; don't be surprised when you see this.

9 Chinese tea is the usual accompaniment to a Chinese meal. It is served without milk, sugar or lemon. When served tea, it is the height of rudeness to leave the cup untouched. At least two sips should be taken. It should also be sipped slowly. The host will be delighted if you praise the tea and accept another cup. (Note: in the old days, business was always conducted with a pot of tea on a side table. After the business was concluded, the host would say, "Let us take tea now," and after drinking, it was the signal to depart. Today, this custom is only practised among members of the older generation.)

The Chinese have a secret that enables them to drink large quantities of alcohol without getting noticeably drunk. They drink one or two glasses of Chinese tea before the festivities. They feel that it helps the absorption of alcohol. Chinese tea is also believed to be very important for digestion when taken with meals, and there is a rumour that Chinese tea, if taken with meals, prevents one from getting fat!

10 Many Chinese do not like iced drinks. They feel that it is bad for the stomach. If you ask for a drink of water in some Chinese homes you may be given hot or warm water—even in the noon-day sun!

Table Etiquette

1 *The Table Setting:* This consists of a pair of chopsticks for each guest, a bowl for rice, a bowl for soup, a small individual dish for the main courses, a dish for bones and other discarded parts, a small dish for soy sauce (a second small dish for preserved cut green chillies may be set), a glass or cup for tea, and a porcelain spoon. A napkin will usually be folded into a clever shape.

2 *Seating.*

 (a) Chinese tables are circular: each guest can speak to· and view each other equally.

 (b) Contrary to Western etiquette, the left side of the host has more honour attached to it than the right side. A woman guest sits to the left, and the man sits to the right of the host. A single guest of honour sits on the left side. The honoured guest usually sits so that he faces the front entrance. Younger guests sit with their back to the front entrance. The reason for this: in the old days, the guest was always allowed to keep his eye on the front entrance in case an enemy should try to attack him. The host sat next to the guest so that he could protect him.

 (c) The host does not take his seat until he has seated everyone at the table. It is polite for him to apologise for the insignificant display and the inferior quality of the food (even if he has taken great pains to ensure that only the best is served). The host may have spent hours and even days discussing the menu with the chef. There is an art in choosing the courses in proper sequence. Spicy dishes must be set off with bland ones, delicate flavours with robust ones, and soft-textured foods should be complemented by crispy food. The perfect dinner guest will stare in amazement as each course is brought in. (The enthusiastic guest will even exclaim "Wah!" at a particularly tempting dish!) He will praise all the subtle nuances and delicate flavours blended into each masterpiece. He may try to guess the ingredients and express pleasure with each mouthful.

3   *Serving and Eating.*
   (a)   Before beginning to eat, the host will invite the guests to drink. This is a form of greeting. The Chinese feel that once the drinking starts, fun and good conversation begins. So even if you do not wish to drink, take a sip or pretend to do so.
   (b)   Do not drink until the host has performed the ceremonial greeting. He will raise his glass and say something like *ch'ing* (please). The guests should raise the glass with two hands, the left hand holding the glass, the fingers of the right hand under the bottom of the glass. Watch the other guests to see how they are holding theirs, and then do the same. (Note: When the host calls for everyone around him to drink together, a chorus of *yam seng* (bottoms up) is appreciated!) Sometimes, after each new course is served, the ceremony is repeated. The Chinese often have games during the meal to induce each other to drink. The losers usually end up by drinking the most!
   (c)   After the first drink, the host will hold up his

chopsticks, repeating *ch'ing*. This is the signal for the guest of honour to begin eating. After the guest of honour has served himself, the other guests begin to eat. The host will usually wait and serve himself last. The rule is "each in his own turn," but it doesn't always happen!

(d) One course at a time is placed in a common serving dish in the centre of the table; there is usually a lazy susan. Be careful when turning it or the dish may land in someone's lap. Watch to see if the other guests have finished serving themselves before turning.

(e) A serving spoon sometimes accompanies each new platter. The guests should use this in dishing out the food. If there is no serving spoon, then use your own chopsticks.

(f) The host may have a special pair of chopsticks that he can use to serve the guest of honour. *If the host places a special tidbit on your plate, you should consider it to be a great compliment.* You can serve the persons seated next to you, or your wife, as a special gesture of courtesy.

(g) Leave the plate on the table while you dish a small portion onto the small plate in front of you. Don't hold it in your hand.

(h) A Chinese feast can consist of up to twelve courses. Pace yourself in the beginning or you may find yourself staggering through the last three or four dishes. The meal is rather like a buffet. Each guest takes just a little bit of all the dishes served.

(i) You should mentally divide the amount of food on the serving platter into the number of guests at the table. Then take only your share, i.e., if eight people are seated, take one-eighth of the amount served.

(j) Always take the piece or pieces closest to you on the serving platter. You should never take the last piece as really polite tables always leave a little bit on the serving dish. (Note: You don't have to eat food that you don't like, but you must eat everything you dish out for yourself. No edible food should be left on your own plate.)

(k) Don't reach across another person's chopsticks while choosing your tidbits.

(l) Rice should be eaten from the little rice bowl. Sauces or condiments can be added to it.

(m) When drinking soup, use your chopsticks to eat the ingredients, but use the soup-spoon to take up the broth. The spoon should be dipped towards you, not away from you as in American etiquette.

(n) Meat or sweet-filled buns should be eaten with chopsticks. The trick is to try and hold the bun on one side with the chopsticks. Take a small bite, then larger ones, until you have eaten your way through the whole thing.

(o) Remove bones or shells from your mouth with your chopsticks. Chicken thighs or wings can be eaten with the fingers. If there is a plate for refuse put the refuse on it. If not, leave them on your own dish and the waiter will usually clear them off before the next course or two.

(p) If the host asks you to have second helpings, it is polite to refuse (so as not to appear greedy). It is acceptable to take more after the host presses it on you. Even if you really don't want any more, it is polite to eat at least a few bites if the host urges you to.

(q) At the end of the meal, place your chopsticks neatly on the table, at the side of your dish. This is a sign that you have had enough to eat.

(r) Chinese tea is served throughout the meal in regular glasses. Beer, brandy or Chinese wine may also be served. Soft drinks are usually available.

Customs and Superstitions Concerning Food

1   Chopsticks are not rested on the dinner plate or rice bowl. They are never laid across them when not in use. They must be placed on a rest stand, the soy-sauce dish or a bone plate. The "handle" portion of the chopsticks sits on the table and the "mouth" portion sits on the rest stand or soy-sauce dish. (Note: It would be embarrassing for the host if a guest laid his chopsticks across the individual plate or rice bowl at the end of the meal. It would be a sign that the guest is still hungry and that the host has not provided enough food.)

2   Never stick a chopstick upright in a rice bowl, not even to chop up something in it. This is a bad omen, as a single chopstick is stuck upright in a bowl of rice at a Chinese funeral to show the separation of the person who has died. The single chopstick is a sign of heaven. It is symbolic of the single joss-stick that is burned for the deceased.

3   Waving chopsticks in the air or pointing with them is bad manners.

4   Slurping soup is considered acceptable. Burping is a sign of appreciation. Westerners should be aware of these customs so they won't be taken by surprise, but they are not expected to follow suit in order to be polite.

5   If any of the guests at the table are seamen, fishermen, or even sailing-boat enthusiasts, a half-eaten fish should not be turned over on the platter. This is supposed to foretell the capsizing of his boat on his next sea trip. The bones can be removed and the fish eaten from the top down.

6   For good luck, the Chinese like to have an even number of guests at a dinner: six, eight, ten or twelve.

Dinner Parties

1   In traditional Chinese practice, dinner speeches are given before the dinner, not after. Don't talk or leave during speeches. Applaud speakers and congratulate them if possible.

Above. These delicious rice dumplings, made with glutinous rice and wrapped in bamboo leaves, are eaten traditionally on the fifth day of the fifth lunar month at the time when the Chinese hold dragon boat races. *Photo: New Nation, Singapore.*

Opposite top. A table placing consists of a bowl for rice, a smaller bowl for soup, an individual flat dish for main courses, a glass for Chinese tea, a little dish for soy sauce or chilli, a porcelain spoon and a pair of chopsticks. Often, though, the bigger bowl is used for rice *and* main courses, with bones and discarded parts going to the flat dish.

Left. *Ch'ing.* The host waves his chopsticks over the yam cake as he invites his guests to join in. One person will break the cake into fairly large pieces with chopsticks, then all will tuck in, picking up the pieces using their chopsticks.

2   At dinner parties or celebrations, all the talk and festivities take place during the meal. Guests do not stay around to chat or drink after supper and tea have been served. *They leave immediately after the last bite or sip has been swallowed!*

3   In a private home, the Chinese may not preface a dinner with a cocktail hour. Among themselves they may serve tea and then follow this with a game of *mahjong* while waiting for the rest of the guests to arrive.

4   Guests do not ordinarily arrive on time for a dinner party. They often arrive thirty minutes to an hour late. The reasons for this are:
(a)   they do not wish to appear greedy
(b)   it is a sign of their importance
It is very likely that this advice about arriving late will be outdated in Singapore in the near future as Singapore is carrying out a "punctuality" campaign to help tidy up the tardiness of its people. However, for the present, I have observed that what people really do and what they think they ought to do are not one and the same thing! The idea that one is advertising oneself as a greedy person by arriving on time will have a hard time dying out. (Note: Promptness is appreciated by restaurant managers as they do not like holding up a reservation for too long.)

5   It is not a good idea to wear white, black or navy blue to a party, as these are traditional colours for funerals.

Restaurant Eating

1   The host usually orders as many dishes as there are guests (with a few extra dishes thrown in for good measure). If there are only a small number of guests, then one or two extra dishes is a must!

2   A good rule while ordering is to include at least one fowl, one fish and one meat dish.

3   Soups can be served at any time during the course of a meal: at the beginning, the middle, and even towards the end.

4   Salads are not served in a Chinese restaurant, but luscious cooked vegetables, crisp and tender, are a necessity.
5   A rice or noodle dish is often served towards the end to make sure that everyone is "filled up".
6   Sweets are not popular after a meal. Fresh fruits or a jellied dessert may be served, but not necessarily. There are no "fortune cookies" in Singapore and Malaysia!

Note: Don't be alarmed at the number of do's and don'ts listed here. The rules are easy to remember after once reading through. They are mostly common courtesy. Chinese meals are good fun, relaxed and pleasurable. The host will be mostly concerned that all the guests are enjoying the food and having a good time. Westerners may look at food differently after having had the experience of visiting or living in Singapore and Malaysia!

PUBERTY

The Chinese do not have a tradition of puberty rituals.

DATING AND COURTSHIP

Among the Chinese of the East, dating is a relatively new innovation. It has not been a common occurrence for more than about twenty years. It has never been a part of their cultural tradition. In the past, matchmakers arranged marriages and horoscope readers and fortune-tellers were consulted to see if they would be successful. Aside from this, polygynous marriages and mistresses were common. (The number of wives a man had were a good indication of his wealth and prestige.) All this is changing today. The young people have been influenced by Western practices through the mass media: television, movies, novels and magazines. They want to have more say in determining their marriage partner.

Multiple wives are no longer allowed, and young Chinese feel that love and affection must play an important role in the relationship. The monogamous marriage—one partner for life, based on "love"—is seen as the ideal. (Note: Muslims are still allowed to have more than one wife.)

The biggest problem, it seems, is how to go about finding a "soul-mate". Indiscriminate dating is frowned on here. The Western practice of dating, where young people are encouraged to meet and mix with many people of the opposite sex before deciding on one particular person, is in direct conflict with traditional Chinese values. Parents would be concerned if their child followed this custom for he would be considered "loose" and a risky marriage partner! On the other hand, if he were to date only one girl, it would be expected to lead to marriage. He is caught in a classic double bind, stuck between the old and the new! The Chinese have had a long tradition of filial respect for their parents. Few of them would go against their wishes openly with regard to courtship and dating. It is rare for a young couple to marry without the consent or blessings of their parents. Compared to Western standards, the Chinese are conservative. Because of these conflicting values, the young Chinese is often confused about whom, when and how to date. He is also confused about what is expected of him on a date. (Westerners are often confused by this too!)

A compromise is generally worked out in this manner: a friend, relative or matchmaker arranges a meeting for the young boy at the girl's home, at a coffee-shop, or at an amusement park. The relatives on both sides are included. The girl can reject the boy then and there, and vice versa, but if everything goes well the boy will be invited to call on the girl at her home. After some time passes, they will be allowed to go to the cinema, etc. If they cultivate a friendship, then the matchmaker/friend/relative can arrange for an engagement. If the friendship does not develop, then no harm is done: the engagement is not forced.

Of course, this pattern has many variations. Some of the more liberal young people, university students, etc., do not follow this practice. They choose their own dating partner and their parents may allow them more freedom. However, in a dating relationship, marriage is usually seen as the end result and virtue is still believed to be a basic value.

Some Patterns of Boy-Girl Relationships

1　A girl does not date until she is about 17 or 18 years old; boys would be a few years older.
2　After a movie, etc., it is common to stop for a light snack at a hawker's stall.
3　The boy "sends her home" (which actually means he escorts her home) at the time her parents have asked that she be in.
4　Kissing is considered bad manners on a first, second or even third date. The couple may know each other several months before their first kiss.
5　Girls are not expected to pay for a boy. "Dutch treats" are also rare.
6　A blind date will always be in a group. If a boy likes a girl in the group and asks her for a date, she must refuse if she doesn't wish to be thought of as "easy". After the group has gone out several more times, he may be allowed to call at her home.
7　Single girls do not go to clubs, discos, etc., without a male escort. They would earn a bad reputation if they did. (European women are often "misunderstood" when they go to a nightclub, restaurant, etc., without escorts!)
8　Boys do not ordinarily pull chairs out for girls, or open doors for them.

ENGAGEMENTS

Matchmaking used to be common among the Chinese of Singapore and Malaysia. Today it is rare. The modern young people prefer to choose their own marriage partners. When a matchmaker is used, she will generally be an old woman and a friend of the family. The parents of a marriageable boy or girl will engage her to find a suitable partner or else send her to approach someone whom they consider suitable. She will be given a nice *hong bao* for a successful match. Chinese are allowed to marry a first, second or third cousin if she is not a daughter of their father's brother. (They would share the same surname, and thus be considered to be of the same blood.) Other cousins are acceptable if they are of the same generation as the young man. Other than that there are few restrictions. Today, first cousin marriages are not encouraged.

The matchmaker will most likely know both the families involved and both families will generally come from the same dialect group and will have equal social standing. In seeking information about the girl, the matchmaker is not above bribing the maid of the girl's family! If everything goes well, photographs will be exchanged and the young man's mother may be taken to meet the girl. Often a meeting between the boy and the girl will also be arranged. A fortune-teller or astrologer will be consulted, and magic tests may be carried out to see if the match will be a successful and harmonious one. Horoscopes are important; a girl born in the year of the tiger is considered a dangerous match for a boy born in the year of the goat; she might devour him. A girl born in the years of the tiger, monkey or snake might have to resort to falsifying her birth year, or else end up a spinster.

Today, matchmakers are still used, but more as a formality. They help with the wedding arrangements. The Chinese do not feel that it is proper for the parents on both sides to engage in direct confrontation over details. Three things take place during a betrothal:

1   The couple exchange rings (or other jewellery).
2   The young man buys special cakes or sweets (a type of peanut brittle or toffee) which are wrapped up in red paper and taken or sent to the friends and relatives of the couple. (In the past, they were only taken to the

bride-to-be's relatives.) When the sweets are received, the friends know that a wedding invitation will soon be on its way. Presents are not sent for the engagement as the wedding will take place shortly. Gifts are taken to the wedding reception.

3   A marriage gift (bride-price) is arranged. This is a symbolic transfer of money from the groom to the bride's parents. It used to signify the transfer of the parents' rights and duties over the girl to her husband. It gave the husband sexual, domestic and procreative rights over his wife. It ensured that the children could bear his surname. It was also a symbolic payment to the girl's parents for bringing her up, washing her nappies, and providing her with day-to-day care. It was never a "dowry" and it did not "buy" a wife. Today, this bride-price is still given and it must be paid up before the actual ceremony takes place. It usually helps to buy the bride's trousseau and bridal furnishings. (Some of the modern young Chinese are dispensing with this custom.)

WEDDINGS

Marriages take many forms in modern Singapore and Malaysia: a church wedding in white for Christians; a civil ceremony or "registry marriage", required by law, but which many Chinese do not feel is as important as the traditional Chinese "tea ceremony" marriage and the new phenomenon of "mass weddings". At a mass wedding, up to 100 couples marry at the same time; there are group rates on the receptions, banquets, and even on the honeymoon.

Until 1960, polygynous marriages were common in Singapore. Some men took as many as seven or eight wives. Only one wife, the first, could be the "primary wife". She could only be a primary wife once in her life, and she had to be a virgin before her marriage. She had priority over any subsequent wives, and they had to show deference to her. The prudent local Chinese kept his wives in separate houses to preserve the peace, unlike his China and Hong Kong brothers who kept them in one villa. A few Chinese did have the ability to keep all their wives "happy" under the same roof and these men were admired, even envied and praised by their friends.

In Malaysia, a bill prohibiting polygynous marriages for all communities (except the Muslim community which is governed by Muslim religious laws) has been passed in Parliament recently but the law is not operative yet. When the Women's Charter came into effect in 1960 in Singapore no new polygynous marriages were allowed, but those who already had multiple wives were allowed to keep them. Besides the polygynous marriages, it was a common and accepted practice to keep mistresses. (I have no new information on whether or not the younger generation follows in the older generation's footsteps in this practice!)

In the past, the bride always went to live in the house of the groom. Her role was to provide children for her husband's male line. She was not considered a full member in the household until she had given birth. Some Chinese couples today make their home with the husband's parents, but many of them prefer to set up housekeeping on their own. Previously, the wedding would last three days, with certain rituals ascribed to each day. Today, the entire ceremony may be telescoped into one day.

Before the wedding, a bridal bed is set up. In order to ensure its power of fertility, a little boy is made to sit or roll on it. Everything in the bridal chamber is new and bright. Red and pink colours adorn the walls, windows, and bedding. The bride's possessions are brought in and everything is made ready. Just before the ceremony, there is a "combing of the hair" ritual in which the boy and the girl, each in their own homes, have their hair ritually combed. The combing is usually done by the mother. This symbolizes the attainment of maturity. (An unmarried person is still considered to be a child—even if he is over forty!)

The bride ordinarily wears a white Western-style wedding

A new innovation in Singapore today! Instead of the traditional practice of placing a little boy on the bridal bed to ensure its fertility, this modern wedding celebration shows a little boy and girl sitting on the bed — this is in keeping with the Singaporean concept of population control: "Two is enough!" *Photo: JoAnn Craig*

dress for the day-time festivities, and changes in the evening to a red or pink evening gown for the banquet. She will have a professional hairstylist and make-up artist attend to her hair and face. The groom wears a smart suit, Western-style, with a shirt and tie.

The groom fetches the bride in a gaily decorated car, festooned with red, pink or gold ribbons and a bride doll

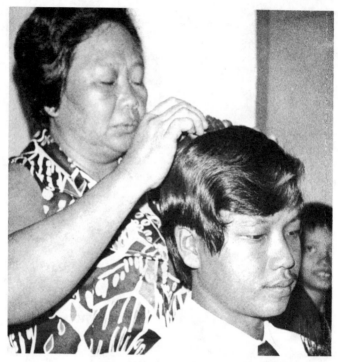

"Today you are a man, my son!" The hair-combing ceremony confers maturity on the young man shortly before he goes through the traditional tea ceremony. He sits before the family's ancestral altar to inform his ancestors of the marriage that is soon to take place.
Photo: JoAnn Craig

attached to the front end. He may bring ceremonial gifts in beautifully-decorated baskets to the bride's family. Some pork, two chickens, two bottles of brandy, red wedding candles, the remainder of the bride-price (if it has not already been paid), clothing, etc. The bride's family returns half of the food and drink to symbolize the unity of the couple. The couple returns to the groom's house, sometimes with gifts of sugar-cane to symbolize sweetness in their life. They may also bring a cock and a hen, given to them by the bride's mother. These are placed under the bridal bed to foretell the sex of their first-born child. (If the cock sticks its head out first, they believe the first-born will be a boy. If the husband hears the cock crow during the night, it means he will have many children! Many young people leave this ritual out of their ceremonies today. In the old days the couple was actually supposed to keep the fowls until they died a natural death. Today they often end up as chicken-rice!)

When the couple reaches the groom's house, the young man aims a well-placed kick at the car door; this is a carry-over from the days when the groom would kick the sedan chair in which the bride was traditionally carried to his house. It symbolizes the authority he is assuming over his wife. At the threshold, the bride steps over a pot of smoking charcoal to cleanse her from evil.

Now, the most important part of the ceremony takes place. On entering the home, the couple pay their respects to the household gods and to the ancestors. They bow three times before the altar to inform the ancestors of the wedding. The tea ceremony follows. *This ceremony traditionally formalizes the marriage!* Two chairs are set up, and the parents of the groom sit on them. The couple offers each parent a cup of tea. The bride and groom are supposed to kneel while offering the tea, but today some couples prefer to remain standing. The father is offered tea first, then the mother. If they take even one sip, it is a sign of acceptance of the bride. If they refuse, it is a sign of rejection and trouble can be expected. This does not happen very often, but if the mother is hesitant, her relatives and friends will urge her to drink it up. The parents replace the tea-cups on the tray that is held by a friend or servant, along with a *hong bao* for the bride. The *hong bao* may contain gold jewellery instead money. It is rare for guests to witness this part of the ritual as usually the family is present. After the parents have been served tea, the senior aunts and uncles, in order of status, come and take their places and continue the ritual.

After these ceremonies, the couple pay a visit to the bride's home. In the afternoon, it is traditional for modern urban couples to visit public parks to pose for photographs. In the evening, a large banquet will be held for all the friends and relatives. It is a festive occasion with hundreds of people in attendance. The bride and groom move from table to table inviting the guests to drink with them. The guests at each table rise to toast the couple, often singing out "Y-A-M S-E-N-G". They hold the notes for as long as possible. Tables often vie with one another to see who can sing the loudest and the longest. There is merry-making, drinking, and eating . . . eating . . . eating!

In theory, the marriage should be consummated on the first night. The bride is not expected to put up a show of resistance, as in a Malay wedding. In the not-too-old days, a specially prepared piece of cloth was laid on the marriage bed and the bride's mother-in-law would inspect it later for signs of virginity. She might test any stain she finds by rubbing lemon juice on it. (If the stain turns yellow after washing, it is genuine.) If the signs were not favourable, the girl might be sent packing with the words "You are not a good girl, go back home to your mother!" The marriage would then be terminated by a divorce rather than an annulment. The Cantonese used to be more specific. It used to be the custom for the groom's family to send a pig to the bride's mother after the consummation. If the bride was found lacking, the pig's ear or tail would be cut off and the mutilated pig paraded to the bride's home—for all the world to see! Today, the older generation is dismayed at the lack of the younger generation's concern for these traditional customs.

Wedding gifts
1 It is customary to give a *hong bao* to the bride and groom.

These red packets are presented at the door.

2   *Hong bao* packets can be purchased at any of the Chinese Emporiums. Be sure to get the one with a "double happiness" sign on the front as there are red packets available for many occasions.

3   The amount given will depend on how well you know the couple getting married. It should always be enough to cover the cost of the meal that you and your partner are eating. Twenty or forty dollars is a normal amount. Whatever you give, it must be given in an even number and in an even amount of bills. So twenty, forty and eighty dollars are lucky amounts. Twenty-five, thirty, thirty-five, fifty, seventy dollars, etc., are unlucky amounts. If you are giving twenty dollars, give two crisp new ten-dollar bills; if you are giving forty dollars, give four ten-dollar bills. (Remember—happiness is born a twin, so give in pairs!)

4   An alternative is to purchase a gift voucher from a department store, or a cash voucher from a bank. They can supply you with the *hong bao* envelope. If you don't know the couple too well, it would be in better taste to offer the voucher rather than cold, hard cash! The amount must still be an even one.

The Reception Banquet

1   It is not polite to arrive on time. If the invitation states 1930 hours sharp, then 2000 hours is a good time for the guests to begin arriving. If a guest shows up at 1930 hours he will find himself sitting alone and advertising himself as a greedy person.

2   Guests leave as soon as the supper is finished and the last drink has been taken. To the Westerner, this seems an abrupt ending to such a festive occasion, but to the Chinese all the festivities should occur during the meal.

3   There may be a lively band and singers to entertain the

guests, but there is usually no dancing at a Chinese wedding.

Dress

1   Wedding suppers are usually a casual affair as far as dress is concerned: short dresses or pantsuits for the women and sports shirts for the men.

2   If the dinner is being held in a smart restaurant or hotel, then the guests should dress more formally: a long skirt for the women, and tie and jacket for the men.

3   Whatever type of dress women wear, colour is important! White, black or navy-blue should be avoided. Un-bleached muslin would mean bad luck for it is often worn to mourn a dead parent. Red, pink or gold are auspicious colours and mean good luck for weddings. (The red colour repels evil spirits: they are said to be afraid of it.)

BIRTHS

A child is considered one year old at birth, and a subsequent year is added at each Chinese New Year. Thus a baby girl born one month before the Chinese New Year celebrations would be considered two years old at the age of four weeks. Western women would certainly frown on this custom!

The most important occasion on the birth of a baby is the "first-month" celebration. A party is held and friends are invited. Good food is served and hard-boiled eggs, with red-stained shells, are distributed. Gifts are given to the baby. This celebration is of great importance for the first son and the first daughter only. Subsequent children will have some ritual, but not the elaborate affair accorded to the first-born. (Sometimes, instead of a party, cakes and red eggs are distributed to friends and relatives at their homes.)

At the "first-month" celebration, the child's hair is ritually cut off. The mother may put it, along with the dried navel cord, into a jar for safe-keeping. When the child is older and begins to argue and fight with his brothers and sisters, the hair will be added to some boiling water, removed, dried off and stored again; The water is given to the child to drink. This is said to stop all future quarrelling. (Note: Of all the mothers I questioned about this, none admitted ever having done this, but they all said that their mother had told them they must do it!) Chinese children are not usually circumcised.

Gifts

1   For a new mother in hospital, a gift of food would be appreciated: a basket of fruit, sweets, cakes, cookies. Bring in pairs.

2   For a new mother at home, a gift of food would also be appropriate: a basket of nourishing delicacies—chicken, eggs, biscuits; milk, noodles, fruit, etc. (She may be on a special diet after childbirth. You can ask what foods she would like.)

3   Flowers would not be appropriate, as the Chinese do not feel that a new mother is ill. Flowers are usually given to sick people or sent to funerals.

4   A gift for the baby: an outfit, matching top and bottom; a baby dress along with a small item like a small toy or a can of baby powder, or a packaged gift set containing nightie, blanket, etc., would be appropriate.

5   A more elaborate baby gift: a gold ring, bracelet or necklace, or a piece of jade, accompanied by a small gift.

6   Always bring gifts in even numbers.

7   For the Chinese, the most joyful colours for gifts are red, pink and yellow.

8   Do not give a woman a gift that has a stork or pictures of a stork on it. In the Hokkien culture, the stork resembles the heron, which is a symbol of death for a woman. It is carried on top of the hearse to show that a woman has died.

FUNERALS

The Chinese religion is a mixture of Buddhism, Taoism and Confucianism. There is a strong belief in after-life and reincarnation. Ancestor worship is of great importance in maintaining family solidarity and the ties between the living and the dead. Reciprocal obligations are set up between the Chinese and their deceased relatives. Obeisance can only be performed by a junior for a senior and thus a young, unmarried boy would be committing an unfilial act if he died before his parents did. After death he would not be venerated at the family altar. A boy who dies young is held to be the reincarnated soul of someone to whom the parents owed a debt; when he dies, the debt is considered paid in full. A dead man will be venerated by his children, nephews, nieces and younger brothers and sisters, but never by his parents. If a man dies without children, his parents must deny that he was their son, or else accept the fact that he is now a "hungry ghost" who must roam homeless without anyone to provide the ritual food and care that he needs in the after-life. However, a man without sons can appoint a nephew as his heir, who must then carry out the rights. If a girl dies unmarried, her family may marry her posthumously so that her tablet can be placed on her husband's family altar. (The spirits of young unmarried girls can be malicious and capricious if not pacified. An unmarried dead son can also be married posthumously; these marriages are called "ghost marriages".)

The prime concern in ancestor worship is with the duties of children in the support and care of their parents, both living and dead. The worst thing a child can do is to neglect his parents by not providing them with food, clothing, shelter and happiness while alive, and ritual veneration and care after death. They must repay the "debt" they owe their parents for the gift of life and the care and support they received as children. In return, the ancestors bless their dutiful children with a prosperous life, children and longevity.

Hungry ghosts can be malicious if neglected. For thirty days (the Chinese seventh month) spirits mingle with humans. The Chinese appease the roaming ghosts with offerings of food, drink, paper money and paper clothes. On the first and fifteenth days burning candles and joss-sticks can be seen flickering and glowing in front of modern HDB flats as well as outside traditional Chinese homes in Chinatown. *Photo: New Nation, Singapore*

Death is marked by lengthy, colourful and traditional ceremonies. It is an expensive affair that can run into thousands of dollars. There are many societies and associations in Singapore and Malaysia whose main purpose is to provide its members with death services. Funerals are sometimes held at home in large open spaces; chairs, canopies and equipment can be rented for this purpose. Alternatively, they are held in funeral parlours. (Not so long ago, Sago Lane, in Singapore's Chinatown, was the centre for "death houses", places where the dying could be taken to await death. This was not a callous act as living conditions were so crowded that it was difficult for a person to find a peaceful place to spend his last days. Aside from this, it was considered bad luck to have someone die in a home where many people were living; his spirit might haunt the premises. Coffin-makers, funeral parlours, florists, paper-house makers, etc., were all conveniently located near by.)

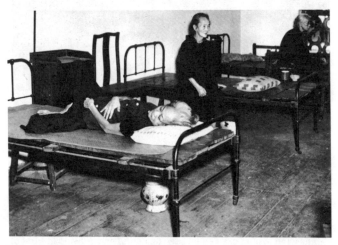

When the "death houses" were situated in Sago Lane, old people like these women came to patiently wait for death. *Photo: Straits Times, Singapore*

After a death, the body is ceremoniously washed, usually by the chief mourner, the man's oldest son. He buys or begs the water as it must not be taken from the house. Two copper coins are thrown into the water to denote purchase. The body is then dressed in an odd number of suits of clothing: three, five, seven or even more. This is to keep it warm on the long journey to the King of Hades. A silver coin is placed between the teeth. This ensures that a gossip will not be reborn at a later time. (Old ladies chide gossipy friends with the remark "You have no silver to block your teeth!") The body is laid out behind a screen; paper money may be burned and offerings placed close by. A chair is also set close by and the deceased's favourite clothes are placed on it. Two candles must be kept burning throughout the period so that the spirit of the dead one can view the surroundings. The priest talks to the body as if it were still alive: "Look, your friends are here to say farewell!" Weeping and wailing starts at a specified time, when it is believed that the spirit of the dead person has returned. This weeping on cue provides a sympathetic welcome to the spirit. The amount and duration of the wailing lets the King of Hades know how much the spirit was loved or hated during his lifetime. Rich families can employ professional mourners to add to the din so the noise will reach the ears of the King of Hades.

Members of the family must keep a constant vigil until the body is buried, sometimes not for three, five or seven days. This vigil ensures that a pregnant cat or rat will not jump over the dead body, thus turning it into a zombie. Friends come to pay their respects and they are given food and soft drinks. They sit around and play mahjong with the mourners to keep them company and help them stay awake. Loud music is played to ward off the evil spirits. Priests light fires and jump through the flames to beat off the evil spirits who lie in wait to capture the soul of the deceased.

On the morning of the funeral, mourners come together for one last gathering. In some funerals stilt-dancers may perform. After the final rites are finished, the mourners accompany the

Above. Chief mourners wear white clothes and sackcloth (symbolic of death); the women wear hoods while the men wear sack-cloth head-pieces. Straw sandals are traditional. Grandchildren wear blue clothes (another symbol of death) but great grandchildren wear red. *Photo: Straits Times, Singapore*

Left. The "cowboy" musicians ride to the funeral in a brightly decorated truck. The clashing of gongs wards off evil spirits along the way. *Photo: Straits Times, Singapore*

coffin to the graveyard. It is an ill omen if the coffin bumps the door posts on the way out. The carriers crowd around it closely and inch it carefully out of the house. This is no easy matter as some coffins can weigh hundreds of pounds. The new high-rise flats provide more difficulties: coffins may not fit into lifts and may have to be carried down fifteen to twenty storeys! A brightly decorated open-sided truck will be waiting and the coffin is placed in it, surrounded by flowers. On top of it there will be a picture of the deceased and a figure of a heron for a lady, or a tiger for a man. A procession forms: first comes the band, wearing fancy costumes, many of which resemble cowboy costumes (the band is usually provided by the clan association of which the deceased was a member), then the priest, the hearse-truck and the mourners. The chief mourners wear sack-cloth over their clothes—the men wear sack-cloth head-bands and the women and children wear sack-cloth hoods. They all wear straw sandals. Grandchildren will have

No, this couple is not performing an extraordinary feat of strength — they have just collected a paper automobile that will be burnt at the rituals for their deceased relative. The essence of the automobile will be mailed to the deceased through the smoke and he will be assured of ample transportation in his new life in the other world.
Photo: New Nation, Singapore

blue tunics placed over the sack-cloth. If there are great-grandchildren, they will be wearing red to symbolize the joy of the deceased in living to a ripe old age! The mourners start off on foot. Automobiles follow to pick up the mourners after they have walked about half a mile. Once the coffin is unloaded at the graveyard, most of the mourners leave and only the deceased's family and close friends remain behind. Several rituals are performed. A priest throws a cock across the open grave, and the chief mourner must catch it. If he succeeds, all is well, but if he misses, misfortune and death will plague the family. Today, many Singapore Chinese are cremated rather than buried as they are running out of burial grounds.

After the funeral (usually seven days after the death), the family burns an elaborate paper and bamboo house complete with paper servants, Sikh watchmen, television sets, automobiles, clothes, jet airplanes, paper opium pipes, and paper money. All these ensure that the deceased will have everything he needs in the after-life. They are "air-mailed" to the deceased through the ritual burning; the essence of the gifts passes through to the spirit world in the flames and smoke. For a specified time after the funeral, the members of the family wear a little patch of coloured cloth on their sleeve.

For the first seven days after death, the soul hovers between the two worlds. Meals will be ritually placed on the altar for the spirit, and on the seventh day it is thought to pay its last visit to its earthly home. During the night, a bed will be made up and a meal set out for it; in the morning, the family looks for signs of the ghostly visit: was the blanket disturbed and were any grains of rice scattered about? On this day, a gravesite visit is paid and all things associated with the dead are burned—the final act of separating the dead from the living! The ancestral tablet is set up, and, from then on, rites will be periodically performed to serve the deceased's needs and gratify his demands. The dead one is the personification of the "family", which goes on and on, and never dies. A hundred days after the death the period of deep mourning is ended. (This period is less than one hundred days if the deceased had sons, for the Chinese subtract the number of sons from the total period of deep mourning. Thus, if there are three sons, the period of deep mourning is ninety-seven days. Daughters are not taken into account when determining the period of deep mourning.) The total period of mourning for parents used to be three years. Today, it is one year. Traditionally, sexual relations and earthly pleasures were forbidden during the period of mourning and a marriage could not be contracted during this time.

Mourning Etiquette for Visitors

1 Visitors usually come in the evening, around 1900 hours.
2 They first pay their respects to the mourners and offer sympathy.
3 A mourner will take the visitor behind the screen where the coffin is placed.
4 The family mourner will kneel and burn joss-sticks. A visitor should stand at the foot of the coffin and bow three times towards it. He need not kneel unless he is a close friend. If a visitor kneels, the mourner must light the joss-sticks for him.
5 It is traditional for the visitor to take some food and drink later. In conversation, a mention can be made of how nice the deceased looks, etc.
6 Visitors should wear dark colours or white. Red, pink, gold and other light or bright colours should be avoided.
7 If you are only going as a tourist to view a mortuary, you should never enter by the front door. This is rude to the mourners.
8 If you happen to pass an outdoor funeral where food is being served, you will be welcomed as the Chinese feel it is good luck and an honour to have many guests at a funeral.
9 On the final day, after the burial or cremation, a large meal is served to the mourners who have accompanied the body to the gravesite or crematorium.

Gifts

1 It is common to give a gift of money to the family. It will help to defray the cost of the funeral and the traditional food and drink.
2 Members of the family and close friends bring their offering in white or brown envelopes. Other visitors may bring their gifts in red packets (so as not to have any of the bad luck attach itself to the giver).
3 For a death, an odd amount of money should be given:

ten, thirty, fifty dollars. An odd number of bills should also be given. If the offering is thirty dollars, do not give it in an even number of bills, e.g. two ten-dollar bills and two five-dollar bills. Give three ten-dollar bills instead.

4   Some Chinese prefer not to receive packets of money. Wealthy families may ask a charitable organisation to set up a table on the premises to receive money from the mourners. They prefer a donation to be given to charity.

5   Flowers can be sent to a funeral.

Leaving a Funeral

1   When a visitor leaves, the family will give him two pieces of red thread or string to keep away any bad luck associated with the death. Just wrap them around a button and throw them away later.

2   The visitor may also be given a *hong bao* containing a single coin—a five- or ten-cent piece. This should be used to buy a sweet on the way home. It will dissociate you immediately from the dead and break any bad luck surrounding the death. Throw away the money if you don't buy the sweet. It should not be taken home. A handkerchief may also be given to mourners who come on the final day.

CHINESE NEW YEAR

Unlike Western celebrations, the Chinese New Year does not last for one night and a hangover. It actually goes on for thirty days. It starts about two weeks before New Year's Eve (the New Year begins on the first day of the lunar calendar and falls anywhere between 21 January and 19 February.) It is the most joyous time of the year for the Chinese. In China, it heralds the beginning of Spring; in Singapore and in Malaysia, it represents a new beginning: a time when all debts are paid up, when all new clothes and shoes must be worn, when the

Chinatown comes alive most especially during Chinese New Year. The streets are crowded with shoppers and hawkers do a thriving business while housewives are prepared to purchase delicacies at inflated prices. Every member of the family must be fitted in new clothes from head to toe. Excitement is so tangible that it can be felt, smelt, tasted and enjoyed. *Photo: Straits Times, Singapore*

entire house must be cleaned and renewed, when old arguments are forgotten and peace restored between family and friends, when the gods and ancestors are worshipped, venerated and propitiated.

All manner of sweets and delicacies must be prepared or bought: waxed ducks, watermelon seeds, groundnuts, sausages, mandarin oranges and many other tasty things. Charm papers, red banners inscribed with lucky words written in gold paint, and garlic cloves must be fastened to the door-frames and outer walls of the house to ward off evil spirits.

Seven days before New Year's Eve, the Kitchen God of each household sets off to visit the Jade Emperor in heaven. It is his duty to report on all the good and evil deeds of the family. (A Chinese husband can always find respite from a nagging wife by going into the kitchen where the picture of the Kitchen God resides. She will not dare nag her husband in

Mandarin oranges, symbol of gold and prosperity, are a must for Chinese New Year. Friends bring them when visiting during the festivities to wish each other good fortune. *Photo: Straits Times, Singapore*

front of the eyes and ears of the Kitchen God!) The family tries to bribe him before he leaves by smearing the mouth of his picture with honey. This ensures that only sweet tales about the family's behaviour are told. Some Chinese say that the honey "gums up" the Kitchen God's mouth so much that he is unable to say anything at all to the Jade Emperor!

On New Year's Eve candles are kept burning all night long; sugar-cane is placed behind a door to make sure that each member of the family has a life that is sweet to the end. Those whose parents are still alive will stay up all night long in the belief that this will add long years to their life. A grand reunion dinner will be held in every house and family members come from near and far to pay their respects to their parents and demonstrate their fealty and devotion.

At 2300 hours (the start of the new morning, according to the Chinese) each member of the family pays homage to the

ancestors at the family altar. After this, the children offer tea to their parents, and the parents offer *hong bao* to the children. Around midnight, a great deal of noise (it used to be fire-crackers before they were banned) is made to scare off any evil spirit that might be lurking around. All the doors and windows are thrown open to usher in the New Year and to greet the benevolent spirits that will bring good luck with them.

On the first, second and fourth days, relatives and friends

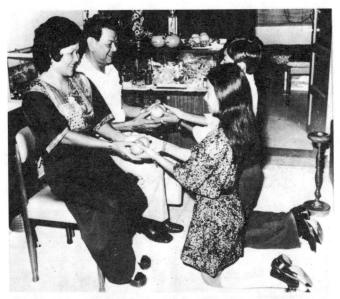

Above. Resplendent in brand new clothes and shiny new shoes, these children pay respects to their parents and offer them oranges. (Note: shoes are not ordinarily worn in an Asian home, but some westernized families may not follow this custom.) *Photo: New Nation, Singapore*

Left. The calligrapher's busiest time of year is during Chinese New Year. Painted lucky charm papers are purchased to repel evil spirits and to bring good luck. The bright red papers with gold characters written on them will adorn door posts and rooms of Chinese homes. *Photo: New Nation, Singapore*

visit each other to eat, drink and wish each other good luck and prosperity. The third day is unlucky for visiting, and many Chinese will stay at home in the belief that quarrels will break out if they don't. The fourth day is a traditional day for businessmen; they usually host a big feast for their employees. On this day, any employee whose services must be terminated will be given notice. Various festivities will go on until the fifteenth day, at which time the New Year celebrations are officially over.

All these *hong bao* packets contain "lucky money". This little one wants his money, but wishes to eat it too! *Photo: Straits Times, Singapore*

Hong Bao

1   It is customary to give your Chinese *amah* or employee a *hong bao*. The red packets can be purchased at any of the Chinese Emporiums. One month's salary should be given if the employee has worked for you at least one year, and two-weeks' salary if less than one year.

2   It is especially auspicious to give *brand new* bills in even numbers and in even amounts: $2, $4, $8, etc. The new bills will prevent anyone from muttering about "old",

"dirty" or "no-good looking" money. These words are unlucky and should not be mentioned during the New Year. They can inadvertently bring on misfortune. In giving *hong bao* to little children, it is permissible to give a one-dollar bill as long as it is accompanied by a ten-cent piece.

3   In Chinese families, the *hong bao* is given to children, unmarried people, members of the family who are younger than the giver, i.e., the grandfather gives to the son and the grandchildren; the son gives to the children— his own and nephews and nieces, etc. This is considered to be lucky money.

4   A *hong bao* should not be given to any government servant, i.e., the garbage collector, the postman, etc.

5   A *hong bao* is ordinarily given to a hairdresser, barber, etc., at this time.

Etiquette during Chinese New Year

During the New Year celebrations, everyone (the expatriates as well as the Indian, Malay and other local communities) is a little bit Chinese. This festival has been included in this book because it is the time of the year when most Westerners come into contact with their Chinese neighbours.

1   It is important to pay up all debts by New Year's Eve. Make sure that you have paid your *amah*, grocer, driver, newspaper delivery man, etc.

2   It is customary procedure to give your Chinese employee four days off during this time. The holiday should begin on New Year's Eve, and last through the third day.

3   If giving a present to someone during this time, give in pairs. Brandy is a favourite gift, but make sure that it is accompanied by something else, i.e. a box of sweets, a brandy miniature, etc. Another favourite gift is a food hamper.

4   If invited to someone's home for tea, etc., it is good manners to bring four mandarin oranges, which are the

colour of gold, for luck and prosperity. They may give two oranges to you in order to return some of the good luck. After taking tea, the visitor should leave a *hong bao* under the cup for the servant.

5   If invited for dinner, a *hong bao* should be left on the last plate at the end of the meal: this is for the servant.

6   Westerners should not visit Chinese friends on the third day of the New Year—the Chinese believe that quarrels will break out on this day. Many Chinese will not have outings on this day in the belief that devils roam abroad.

7   When visiting a Chinese friend during the New Year do not wear black. It is supposed to bring bad luck.

8   If you cannot visit Chinese friends or business associates during the first fifteen days, be sure to ring them to wish them "*Gong Xi Fa Cai*" ("Good Luck and Prosperity").

Taboos and Superstitions about the New Year

1   No unlucky words must be spoken during the New Year festivities.

2   Brooms must not be visible or used or else good luck will be swept away.

3   Nothing in the home should be broken. Be very careful when handling cups, glasses, and especially mirrors. If anything, especially a mirror, is broken, it means the family will split up or a death will occur in the family.

4   No old clothes should be worn.

5   Needles and scissors should not be used for they are believed to bring bad luck.

6   Children may not be punished or scolded on New Year's Day.

7   Washing the hair is considered unlucky during this time. It washes away good luck!

8   Rain on New Year's day foretells a year without drought.

9   A gambling win foretells similar good fortune for the coming year.

4 The Malay Community

THE PEOPLE

Fifteen per cent of the people of Singapore and fifty-three per cent of the people of Malaysia are Malays. The Malays are a gentle people. Courtesy, etiquette and good manners form an essential part of their everyday life. These values are reflected in the way they treat each other and in the way they treat strangers—with respect and consideration. Few visitors can leave a Malay community without being over-whelmed by the kindness that is shown to them. Malays have a "community spirit". Friends, relatives and neighbours feel a responsibility to help each other in times of joy, need and grief.

While urbanization and modernization have changed the life-styles of many of the Malay people of Singapore and Malaysia, the community as a whole has preserved its values and traditions. The younger generation, while more "up-to-date" than their parents, still adheres to the age-old traditions of hospitality, courtesy and etiquette that form an essential part of the Malay personality. The Malays in Singapore and Malaysia are Muslims; it is their religion that shapes the foundation of their everyday lives. Being Muslims, the Malays are expected to recite the creed: "There is no God but Allah, and Mohammed is his Prophet"; pray five times a day and worship Allah as the one true God; practise charity and help the needy; fast during the month of Ramadan; and, if possible, make a pilgrimage to Mecca at some time during their lives. By religious law, certain things are *haram* (forbidden): hence, Muslims must abstain from pork and alcohol and some other foods, and they must not come into contact with the nose, wet hair or lick of a dog. It is also *haram* for women to sit together with men in the main part of the mosque, to casually touch members of the opposite sex, and to wear immodest clothing. There are also certain other things which are *makruh* (allowed but not encouraged), for example, smoking, and eating crabs or shellfish.

According to Dr Tham Seong Chee of the Department of Malay Studies at the University of Singapore, the ethical system of the Malay people revolves around the concept of *budi*. This is the ideal behaviour expected of them. It reflects the degree of character and breeding within each individual. The rules of *budi* are: respect and courtesy (especially towards elders), affection and love for parents, a pleasant disposition, and peace and harmony in the family, neighbourhood, and society as a whole. There are two forms of *budi*:

1   *Adab* (this is on the individual level): the individual has a responsibility to show courtesy in word, deed, and action to all people at all times; and

2   *Rukun* (this is on the social level): the individual must act to obtain harmony, whether it be in the family, community, or in society.

The concept of *budi* can be seen as "the internalization of the social conscience of the individual. It is the measure of the nobility of his character. One's name and status in society is concomitant with one's *budi*."*

---

*   Tham Seong Chee, Ph.D., "Tradition, Values and Society Among the Malays", *Nanyang Quarterly,* Vol. 1, No. 4 (December 1971), pp. 12-13.

This child's face is a reflection of the love and respect that Malay children feel for their elders. Children are treated gently and tenderly in the Malay community. *Photo: Times Publishing, Singapore*

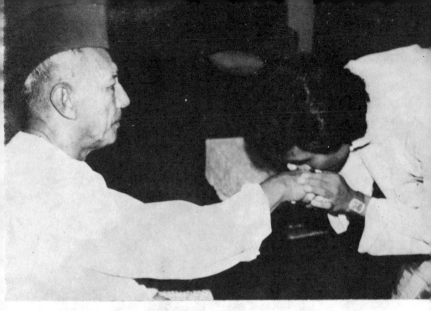

A young man *ciums* his grandfather's hand. This gesture is a request for the blessing of his elder. The young Malay will repeat this *cium* whenever he leaves his home or prepares for a journey. *Photo: JoAnn Craig*

While Malays as a whole do not value the pursuit of wealth, power and prestige for their own sake, they do firmly believe in industry, hard work, and self-reliance. They feel that life is a fleeting thing, and that responsibility to family, friends and the community takes precedence over self-centred interests, i.e. profit accumulation and materialism. In other words, "people are more important than possessions"!

The Malays love children. They raise them gently and tenderly. Perhaps the best indication of the Malay spirit is seen in the way they raise their children. Babies are cuddled and loved. (Parents don't kiss their children; they *cium* them, i.e., they place the side of their nose against the child's cheek and give a little sniff! Indeed, a Western kiss is considered quite humorous to the Malays!) The Malay father plays as much of a role in rearing them as the mother. The father spends a great deal of time holding them, playing with them, carrying them about, and rocking them to sleep. If a

Malay father sits down for a minute's rest, a little child will surely find its way into his arms. A youngster is taught by example and praise; physical punishment is frowned upon. Respect between parents and children is reciprocal. Westerners will be touched by the consideration shown to parents by their children.

Malay women are decently, modestly, but attractively dressed. Their customary costume covers the whole body except for the face, hands and feet. Even today, in modern cities like Singapore and Kuala Lumpur, it is common to see Malay women in their *baju kurung* (a long-sleeved overblouse covering a *sarung*). A married woman often wears a *sarung kebaya* (a close-fitting lace overblouse over a *sarung*). (An appreciative Malay will say that she has a shape "like a guitar"!)

Because Malay women must sit apart from the men in the main portion of a mosque, and are not allowed to mix casually with men, or to eat with them, people may think that they are downtrodden. This is not true. The older a Malay woman gets, the more self-possessed she becomes. Malay women enjoy being women. They are strong and reliable, and they have no fear of hard work (especially those from the state of Kelantan in Malaysia). They have a love of gold jewellery. Extra money spent on gold necklaces, bracelets, etc., is considered to be a good investment. (This is something they have in common with Indian and Chinese women). The amount of a woman's gold is a good indication of her husband's wealth. The Malay husband may make major decisions, but his wife exercises a great deal of influence. She does in fact wield power in her society. She is definitely not an oppressed person; she gives deference and respect to her husband, love and compassion to her children, but she is still very much her own person!

In the etiquette that follows, I have given mostly *rural* customs as so many visitors to Singapore and Malaysia will have an opportunity to travel through the rural parts of Malaysia. Urban Malays also practise much of this same etiquette themselves, but the more modern and Westernized Malays often adapt themselves to Western manners and courtesy when meeting and mixing with European friends and visitors. Where the practice differs between rural areas and urban areas, they will be noted.

LEARNING TO SOCIALIZE

Introductions
The basic rules are the same as for the Chinese, i.e., the elder should be mentioned before the younger, the more important before the less important, the woman before the man, etc.

Salaming or Shaking Hands
1   *Men and women in rural areas:* It is not customary for men and women to shake hands with each other. Malay women may *salam* with men *if* they cover their hands with a cloth. (The reason for this is that men have to ritually cleanse themselves before praying if they come into contact with women, and vice versa.)
2   *Men and women in cities:* Malays shake hands with both men and women if they feel that the person is unaware of the social etiquette pertaining to handshaking. (They would rather break their own rule than hurt the other's feelings!) Some Malays of the younger generation shake hands freely with members of the opposite sex. However, it would be more polite for a Western woman to acknowledge an introduction with a Malay gentleman with a nod of her head and a smile. The Malay is pleased if the Westerner cares enough to learn their custom of *salaming* with members of the *same* sex.
3   *Salam—men with other men:* This traditional Malay greeting resembles a handshake with both hands but without the grasp! The man offers both hands to his friend, lightly touches his friend's outstretched hands,

"I greet you from my heart." After softly touching hands, the women bring their hands to the breast in an embracing motion. Notice that the younger woman uses both hands, the older only one. *Photo: JoAnn Craig*

then he brings his hands to his breast. (This means simply: "I greet you from my heart.") It is done with both hands to show greater deference, i.e. with older people. Between younger men, it may be done more casually, with one hand.

4   *Salam—women with other women:* Women can use the form mentioned above, but in rural areas there is a slightly different version. The women sit down first, knees to one side, both feet tucked under the body, away from view. They lightly touch the hands of their friend between their hands then bring their hands up to their face, covering the nose and mouth in a gesture that could be analogous to the prayer position of the hands. They then touch their breast with their right hand. This can also be done while standing. The general meaning of this *salam* is "I kiss the greeting and accept it through my mouth and down into my heart."

Greetings

1   In rural areas, it is the habit of friends meeting in public to greet each other with: "Where are you going?" The answer to this is "For a stroll" or "Nowhere of importance". This greeting does not mean that the Malays are curious about your comings and goings; it is just their polite form of greeting. It is similar to the Western "How are you?" "Fine, thank you". Another greeting that is commonly used is: "I wish you peace and tranquility *(Selamat sejahtera ke atas anda.)*" Today, many urban Malays greet each other with "How are you?" as well as the more usual "Where are you going?"

2   In greeting a Malay friend, it is good manners to inquire about the family, their health, the children, etc.

Names

1   Most Malays trace their descent through their fathers, but they do not have surnames. They tack their father's name onto the end of their own name. This name only lasts for one generation.
    Example:

> Grandfather: Isa bin Aman
>
> Father: Osman bin Isa
>
> Son: Ali bin Osman

2   Some Malaysians trace their descent through the female line (the Minangkabau people) but this is not common in Singapore.

3   An explanation of a Malay man's name.
    Example: Isa bin Aman.
    (a)   *Isa* is the individual's name. His friends call him Isa. Westerners can call him Mr Isa. His Malay address is "Encik Isa".
    (b)   *bin* means "son of".
    (c)   *Aman* is the father's name. It is not a surname.

(d) The modern practice is to drop the *bin*. Thus, Isa bin Aman may be simply called Mr Isa Aman.

4 An explanation of a Malay woman's name. Example: Zaitun binti Abdullah (married to Isa bin Aman).

(a) *Zaitun* is the individual's name. Her friends call her Zaitun. Westerners can call her Mrs Zaitun Isa. Malays would call her Puan Zaitun (*Puan* is the term for a married woman).

(b) *binti* means "daughter of".

(c) *Abdullah* is her father's name. It is not a surname.

(d) A woman does not necessarily take the name of the husband when she marries. Traditionally, she could retain her father's name. The modern practice, however, is to drop the father's name and to attach the husband's name, as in Mrs Zaitun Isa Aman. When in doubt how to address a Malay friend, ask.

SOME COMMON COURTESIES AND CUSTOMS

Clothes

Hot summery days in this equatorial region go well with sleeveless blouses and backless dresses; but, if you are visiting an urban Malay home or a Malay rural community, please dress modestly. In the towns and *kampungs* (villages) of Malaysia, do not wear skimpy clothes of any kind. Malays take their religion very seriously; modest dress is part of their religious culture. Visitors to Malaysia should respect their customs and beliefs and they should not cause embarrassment by exposing parts of their body publicly. Clothes that should not be worn by women while visiting the Malay home, or in public in Malaysian communities, include: shorts, cut-offs, mini-skirts, bikinis, halters, shirts and dresses without bras and dresses which expose the armpits.

Dogs

Muslims are not allowed to come into contact with the wet nose, wet hair, or the lick of a dog. They especially don't like to have a dog leap or jump on them. This is a religious restriction. (You will see a lot of cats in a Malay village, but dogs are a rarity.) If a Muslim visits you in your own home, it is a good idea to keep your dog in another room.

Gambling

Malays are not supposed to gamble; although they may play cards and other games as a pastime, they are not allowed to gamble for money.

Gestures and Touching

1 It is not good manners to point to a place, object or person with the right forefinger; you can point with the thumb of the right hand, the four fingers folded under.

2 If you want to beckon a person or a taxi to you, use the four fingers of the right hand, fingers moving together with the palm facing down. Use a waving gesture.

3 The Australians have a gesture to indicate "drinking up": the first three fingers of the hand are folded to touch the palm, and the thumb and little finger are extended straight up. This gesture may be offensive to older Malays. The thumb is a symbol of God and the little finger is a symbol of evil. Some Malays could literally take this to mean "God is evil". Take care not to make this gesture in front of older Malays or their families.

4 Your friend has a beautiful child with soft brown eyes and a dimpled smile! Restrain your impulse to pat him on the head. The head is considered to be the seat of intellectual and spiritual powers. It is sacred and mustn't be touched. It is permissible to pat him on the chin, with the right hand! In urban areas, the younger Malays may not be aware of this taboo on head patting, but it is inadvisable to do it anyway!

"Let's have another beer." This gesture should never be made in front of older Malays as it could be taken to mean "God is bad". Note: Alcoholic drinks are *haram* for Muslims. *Photo: JoAnn Craig*

5   While holidaying in Malaysia, especially in the rural areas, please don't walk down the street holding hands, or draping your arms around each other (for boy-girl relationships only). There are legal restrictions against Muslims kissing, hugging, etc., in public. Malays expect men and women to conduct themselves with decorum and dignity. Even married couples are careful to observe this rule.

6   Remember the rule about casual touching between members of the opposite sex. Men, do not lay your hands on a woman! Women, do not lay your hands on a man! This holds true for clerks in shops, waitresses in restaurants, etc. It is also applicable in Singapore.

Mosques

1 Non-Muslims may visit a mosque during organized prayer, but they must be quiet and respectful. Services take place on Friday afternoons.
2 Shoes must always be removed. Muslims wash their feet before entering.
3 The Muslim must step over the threshold with his right foot first.
4 Do not cross in front of the people who are praying at any time.
5 Do not enter the part of the mosque that is called the "Mehrab".
6 Women must not enter a mosque with the knees and arms exposed. Modest dress should be worn.
7 Women, even non-Muslim women, must not enter a mosque while they are menstruating.
8 Ask for permission before taking photographs.
9 Do not touch the Koran (Holy Book).
10 Muslim women do not enter a mosque for 44 days after childbirth.

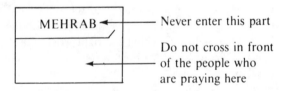

Top. As dawn begins to break, a Muezzin announces the Call to Prayer. Muslims pray five times daily: at dawn, noon, before and after sunset, and before retiring. *Photo: Times Publishing, Singapore*

Bottom. Before praying in a mosque, the Muslim woman covers her body with a *telekong*. This garment covers the entire body (including the head and hair), leaving only the face and the two hands up to the wrists exposed. *Photo: Straits Times, Singapore*

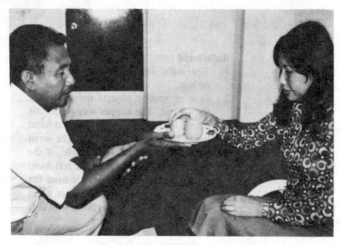

The polite way of handing an object to someone is to hold it in the right hand while lightly touching the right wrist or forearm with the left. *Photo: JoAnn Craig*

Right hand

1   The right hand only is used while eating.
2   Give or receive objects only with the right hand. The proper way to do this is to give the object with the right hand while lightly touching the right wrist with the left hand. (Of course, if the object is too heavy, then the left hand must help!) The left hand is used for hygienic purposes (washing after using the toilet). To offer anything with it is insulting!

Smoking

While Muslims do not have religious restrictions against smoking, it is considered commendable for them to refrain from it. Ask for permission before smoking in a Malay home. In Singapore, the rule is the same when elders are present. The younger generation are not so concerned about guests smoking.

ON BEING A HOUSE GUEST

Adab of Host and Guest

1   According to Malay *adab*, the host assumes the responsibility for the well-being of his guest. He makes every effort to show hospitality for it is a reflection of his good name and character.

2   Since the guest puts himself entirely in the hands of the host for the duration of his visit, it is proper for him to inform his host before he does anything independently, e.g., before leaving the house, shopping, etc.

Shoes

1   Shoes must always be removed when entering a Malay home. This has to do with their ritual taboos. Shoes may have come in contact with something considered "unclean", like dog excreta. Do not wear them on the porch either.

2   If the host tells you that you can leave your shoes on, check to see if the members of the family are wearing them, then do as they do. The family may wear special slippers in the home. Do not mistake them for shoes!

3   In a *kampung,* leave the shoes on the steps outside the home.

4   In a flat leave the shoes outside the front door, to the right or left: do not block the entrance.

5   For hygienic purposes, people in rural and urban areas are encouraged to wear sandals or shoes outdoors.

6   In some rural areas, there may be a jug of water on the porch to wash the feet with. However, this is not common today, as even rural Malays are careful to wear shoes when not in the house.

Feet

1   The soles of the feet should not be exposed. A Western businessman should never put his feet up on his desk in

front of a Malay businessman for this causes grave insult.

2 Malays consider it impolite to point their feet at anyone (as one would point the finger at a person). This does not mean that one cannot point one's feet in the direction of someone while walking or standing.

Sitting

1 Many Malay homes have Western-style chairs and sofas; but people often sit on colourful mats on the floor. Do not sit down at the first available place; wait until your host invites you to sit and indicates a place for you. Do not step over a person who is seated on the floor. People do not generally sit with their legs outstretched before them.

2 When sitting on a chair, Malays do not cross their legs if older or respected persons are present. This is true for both rural and urban areas.

3 When sitting on the floor, the rules may vary in urban and rural areas:

   (a) In rural areas, men sit cross-legged. Women always sit with their knees to one side and the feet tucked under them, *away from view.*

   (b) In cities, the above holds true for formal occasions, weddings, etc. But if one is at a friend's home (and elders are not present), then it is permissible for men and women guests to sit with the knees up, down, or sideways.

4 In rural areas, don't offer a cushion used for the head to a Malay to sit on. Malays feel it will "raise a boil on the buttocks"! The Indians and Chinese also would not sit on something meant for the head.

General

1 A guest in a Malay home should never sit or stand on the prayer rug. (A casual visitor may not see the prayer rug, but a house guest may!)

2 A guest should not ask to touch the holy book (Koran).

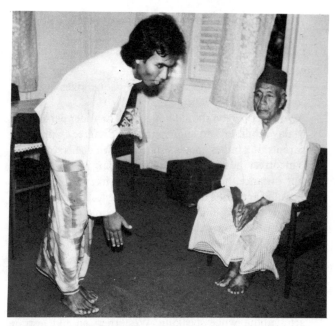

The well-bred Malay guest never passes in front of a person without making this polite gesture. *Photo: JoAnn Craig*

The Muslim must purify himself before he can touch it.

3   It would be considered good manners if the woman guest offered to help her host's wife with some of the household chores.

4   The Malay family will appreciate it if the guest gets up with the family and does not sleep in late.

5   The polite guest will always be careful when he crosses in front of another person. There is a proper way to do it. Bend over slightly from the waist, extend the right hand in front of you, touch the right wrist with the fingers of the left hand, then say "May I please pass." It is rude to cross in front of another person without using these words and this gesture.

6   Women should always dress modestly while visiting or
     staying in a Malay home.

Conversation
1   There should be no "sex talk" or risque jokes in mixed
     company.
2   A younger person should not correct an older person and
     Malay children do not publicly disagree with their
     parents. If a father makes a statement which his son thinks
     is incorrect, he will be courteous in asking for clarification.
     For instance, he may say something like "I think it was
     Tuesday and not Thursday when the guests arrived. What
     is your opinion, father?" Younger people are concerned
     that the older ones should not "lose face". They try never
     to embarrass them.
3   Young people do not join in the discussion very much
     when elders are present. They tend to listen attentively.
4   Malays have gentle ways. They do not laugh loudly or
     speak harshly. They do not gesture wildly or wave their
     arms about while speaking. Westerners should restrain
     themselves when in the presence of elders, so they won't
     appear to be coarse. The younger generation (when elders
     are not present) are more uninhibited in cities than in
     rural areas!

Bathing in Rural Areas
Men and women bathe separately at an outdoor well. Guests
should bathe at least twice a day.
1   Women wear a *sarung* wrapped around the body,
     covering the chest and the knees. One dips water from the
     well using the bucket that is provided. (A rope is usually
     attached to the bucket for the purpose of hauling the
     water up.) The *sarung* is not removed while soaping or
     rinsing the body. The water is poured over the body and
     down the front and back of the *sarung*. Their hair is
     usually washed every day. A dry *sarung* is slipped over

Bathing at an outdoor well is cool and refreshing. Women wear a *sarung* at all times while splashing water over and through the *sarung*. A dry *sarung* is slipped over the head and secured before the wet one is released.

the wet one and the latter is removed before returning to the house.

2 Men wear a man's *sarung* wrapped around the waist. Do not bathe with just a swimsuit or a pair of shorts on.

3 It is not polite for men to watch women bathing.

4 Do not drop soap suds, toothbrushes and bathing articles into the well for the same water may also be used for drinking purposes (after boiling). Malays are very careful to keep their well water pure and clean. They must bathe with clean water (to ritually purify themselves) before praying. Visitors, please be careful not to contaminate the water!

5 If the bucket should fall into the well, it can be fetched out with a long stick with a hook at the end. There should be one around the area, perhaps under the eaves of the house.

Bathing in Urban Areas

If a shower is not available, then there will probably be a bucket of water and a scoop for rinsing purposes.

Toilet Facilities

In rural areas, there is usually an enclosed squat-type toilet a short distance from the house proper. Bring a bucket of water from the well into the toilet with you. It is considered cleaner to wash with water than to use toilet paper. It is also a religious obligation. (In any case toilet paper may not be available.) The left hand can be used *now!* Once you have used your left hand for this purpose you will understand the Malays' (and the Indians') reluctance to use it for social purposes! In urban areas, there is usually a squat-type toilet indoors. The cleaning procedure is the same.

Leaving

When the visit is over, the guest should ask the host for permission to leave the house before he departs. In Malay, the guest literally asks: "May I take back myself now?" In urban homes, the guest can say "May I leave now?" or "I'd like to leave now."

Bread-and-butter gifts

1   The thoughtful house guest asks to help the wife with the shopping: "Can we shop together?" The host will not expect the guest to buy groceries, but it is a nice gesture on the part of the guest to offer.

2   It is insulting to offer money to your Malay host.

3   If bringing gifts for the family, it is a good idea to bring them with you, rather than to purchase them at the local shops. (In rural areas, you may not be able to find a wide variety of merchandise at the local shops.)

4   Present the gifts to the family on departing, not on arrival.

5   In rural areas, a much appreciated gift is some Indonesian batik for the hostess. This may sound like bringing ice to the Eskimos or coal to Newcastle, but batik is very important to the Malays. It plays a part in almost every phase of their lives. It is used as a *sarung,* a sling or swing for the baby, a bathing costume, a sleeping gown, and, finally, as a shroud. Bring the best pieces you can find in lovely red, orange or green. The dark and sombre colours (brown, grey or navy blue) should be avoided. White, the colour associated with funerals, should also be avoided. Your hostess will be delighted with batik. She can usually tell its quality by smelling the wax in it. It will probably be used for a very special occasion!

6   Some other nice gifts are perfumes and colognes for the hostess and toys for the children. Malay children are loved and petted. Any consideration you can show to them will endear you to the Malay heart.

7   Malay men would appreciate nice cotton shirts with collars and a cotton man's *sarung* in stripes or plaids. (Men ordinarily like to wear new ones for prayers!)

8   In urban areas like Singapore, Indonesian batik is not such an auspicious gift as it is readily available. Modern urban Malays are also not too concerned about avoiding dark colours and white. An appropriate gift would be something for the home, or a souvenir from the guest's native country.

Gifts in General

1   Malays accept a gift with pleasure and may give one in return. If a Malay hostess gives some item of her own clothing, e.g. a *baju kurung,* it means she is treating the guest as one of the family, and that she is paying special honour to the guest.

2   Malays do not feel it is polite to open a gift in front of the giver. The host will express delight, show the package to his wife, then he may set it aside until they are alone. Even children may be careful not to open a gift in company.

3   There are no hard and fast rules on the kind of gift to give to a Malay. One should remember, however, the restrictions on Muslims: no pork, no liquor, no ashtrays, no personal items (like underwear), no knives, no toy dogs, etc.

FOOD AND DRINK

1   It is absolutely *haram* (forbidden) to eat pork as it is considered to be unclean. It will never knowingly be touched, served or eaten. If you have a Malay *amah*, it would be most improper to insist that she prepare pork, bacon, ham, etc.

2   Muslims also have religious restrictions against eating any meat (beef, lamb, chicken, etc.) that has not been slaughtered by a Muslim. When serving meals to Muslim guests, it is polite to inform them that the meat has been specially purchased and conforms to their standards.

Mutton and beef sold at *government markets* conform to Muslim standards. Meat packages in supermarkets that conform to Muslim standards will have the word "Halal" printed on it and a green crescent and star visibly displayed. Slaughtered chicken would have to be bought from a Muslim; live chickens may be bought from anyone but would have to be slaughtered by a Muslim after the ritual prayers. Your provisioner can supply you with meat that conforms to Muslim standards if you make a special request.

3   Some other foods that may not be served to a Muslim are: amphibious animals like the frog and duck; carnivorous animals and birds like tiger, bear, eagle and shark; creeping and crawling animals like snakes and lizards; squirrels and guinea-pigs.

4   Foods which come under the *makruh* (not encouraged) category are crabs and other shelled seafood. Some Muslims will not eat these foods so it is best to find out if your Muslim guests can eat these before you invite them for a meal!

5   Alcoholic drinks are also *haram*. Have soft drinks available for your Muslim guests. Do not expect to be served alcohol in a Muslim home.

6   Malays are generally not fond of Western cheeses and sweets after a meal. However, the *adab* of the Malay is such that he will adapt himself to any food the host offers him, so long as it does not contradict his religious obligations. He will at least try a little of whatever is served.

7   The foods which they generally *do* like are foods with a fish-paste *(belacan)* flavouring or anchovy flavouring, spicy, curried foods, green cooked vegetables, and especially chicken. (Chicken is usually served to honoured guests.) They also like fruit after a meal and unsalted rice.

8   Always offer a Malay visitor some refreshments. The polite host will invite the guest to eat with the request

"Please eat," or something similar. It is a custom for the Malay to wait for this invitation before he begins to eat or drink.

9   A dish of salt on a Malay table is more than a dish of flavouring. It is a symbol of friendship. If the host offers you salt from the dish, dip the forefinger of the right hand in and taste it. It cements your friendship. (Note: Salt is offered to a *bomoh* (a local shaman), after he has performed some spiritual or physical healing on a person; the salt replaces the strength and power he has expended in the curing process. A student offers salt to his teacher at the end of a course of instruction to replace the knowledge the teacher has given of himself. A new baby is often offered a taste of salt when he visits a Malay home with his parents for the first time. The lady of the house puts a dab on his tongue. The salt symbolizes strength and wisdom. It is never asked for by the teacher, *bomoh,* etc.; it should be given freely by the person who has received the service.)

Table Etiquette
1   *The Table Setting*
  (a)   In rural areas, food and refreshments may be served to guests while they sit on mats on the floor.
  (b)   Modern urban Malays usually have a Western table setting. Forks and spoons may be placed at the side of the Westerner's plate of rice, but there will be no knives. Knives are considered by some Malays to be weapons and hence are not used at the table. Another explanation for the absence of knives at the table may be that they are just unnecessary since the meat is usually cut into bite-size pieces before cooking.
  (c)   A glass of water or juice is set on the left side of each plate of rice. The left hand is used to handle the glass since the right hand is normally soiled from eating.

Serving platters or bowls are set in the centre of the table.

2   *Seating*

   (a) Often refreshments or meals are served to guests while they sit on colourful mats on the floor. This custom is more often seen in rural areas.

   (b) The guest of honour will usually be placed at the head of the table. He may alternatively be placed at the right side of the host. '

   (c) In rural areas, men and women do not sit together for meals. The women serve the men first, and eat after the men have finished. Out of courtesy to male and female guests, especially Western ones, the Malay host may invite both men and women to eat at the same table. In this case, women sit on the left side of the host, and/or on the left side of the men (clockwise).

   (d) In traditional homes, the host or hostess may not join the guests for refreshments or a meal. This enables him to give his full attention to the guests and enables his wife to be ready to serve the guests' needs. The manner in which the host gives his full attention to the guests is worthy of note. The host sits forward, in a very alert manner, watching the faces of his guests closely. He gives one the impression that what is being said is of the utmost importance and deserves quiet, considerate attention.

   (e) In modern homes, the host or hostess often joins the guests for meals.

3   *Methods and manners in serving and eating*

Many of the customs given below are traditional ones *closely* followed in the pattern of dining in rural areas. In modern cities, many of the young Westernized Malays may not expect their guests to be conscious of this etiquette. Indeed, some of the younger ones may not be aware of it themselves! However, if you are planning a visit with a Malay family, it is wise to understand these customs so that you can join the family and not set yourself apart from them. The Malay host will be genuinely pleased if the guest takes the time and effort to learn his customs. Many mistakes will be forgiven the considerate guest; the fact that one is *trying* is enough to to warm the Malay's heart!

(a)   Malays are quick to show hospitality to a guest by offering food and drink. The guest must not absolutely refuse any food or drink that is offered. Only a little bit need be taken if one is not hungry. In rural areas, the refusal of food or drink could be a sign of fear that something may have been added to it to cause illness, or that some sorcery has been performed on it. In modern Malay society, the refusal of food or drink is not seen so much as fear of sorcery, as a case of bad manners.

(b)   If it is absolutely necessary to refuse food offered (because of sickness, special diet, allergy, vegetarian proclivity, etc.) then you should explain the reasons. In rural areas, food can be refused without giving offence if the guest touches the bowl or jug which holds the food offered with the forefinger or thumb of the right hand. (In the old days this was done to appease the spirit of the food offered; without this appeasement, the spirit might be offended and cause some misfortune to befall the offender.) In modern society it is only necessary to explain why the food or drink cannot be taken. If possible, just break off a small piece of the cake, cooky, etc., and nibble it. The Malays have a saying that goes "Never refuse food or drink with your face; refuse with your mouth." This means that you should never "make a face" or show an unsightly grimace when refusing what is offered.

The right hand should be washed before beginning to eat. Here, the host washes his guest's hand with water from a special utensil. The Malay host may offer a small fingerbowl and towel instead. (Note the correct way to sit on the floor: the lady tucks her feet to the left while the man sits cross-legged.) *Photo: JoAnn Craig*

(c) The Malay hostess may offer a small towel and a bowl of water to the guests to wash their hands in before the meal. Do not mistake this for soup!

(d) Traditionally, Malays do not eat with fork and spoon. They use the fingers of the right hand. Forks and spoons may be offered to Western guests, but it's good fun to try your luck using the fingers instead. The most proper way to eat with the fingers is to scoop up a little food in the hollow created by holding and bending the fingers together. Do not get the palm soiled. Bend over the dish slightly and,

The right hand only is used for eating. Food is held in the curve of the fingers and is gently pushed into the mouth with the thumb. *Photo: JoAnn Craig*

using the thumb, push the food into the mouth. The tongue should be slightly sticking out to receive the food. Do not suck it into your mouth or make sucking noises! Sucking or licking of fingers is considered bad manners.

(e) The left hand may be used for serving and passing dishes of food, and for holding a glass. When passing a serving dish that is too heavy, hold it in the left hand and support it with the back of the right hand. This is allowed as the right hand will be soiled from eating. If Westerners are using fork and spoon, they should use the customary right hand for serving and holding the glass.

(f)   Food is passed around the table from right to left.

(g)   The food is usually served in common serving dishes. Each person helps himself to a little, using the serving spoon. Be careful not to touch the food on your plate with the serving spoon. Drop or pour the food onto your rice or dish.

(h)   The host or hostess may serve the guest and they ordinarily love to dish out generous portions! If given too much rice, make sure that you replace the unwanted portion back into the serving dish *before* you begin to eat, or you will be obliged to eat it all. (Do this only if your plate is clean and the rice has not been covered by gravy or other foods. When refusing second helpings, spread your hand over your own plate and say "no thank you" or something similar.)

(i)   Before eating or drinking, it is polite to wait until the host asks you to accept it, even if it is set before you! It is also customary for the guest to invite the host to join him before he begins to eat. Raise the cup or dish (put the plate on the flat of the left palm and hold it out with the right hand), gesture towards the host and say "Will you please join me?" The host may then ask the guest to "please carry on". This is the sign for the guest to begin!

(j)   Malays—in fact, most Asian races—do not like wasting food. Dropping food on the table or floor is like throwing away one's livelihood. Be careful not to do this. At the end of the meal, the plate should be clean to show that one has had enough. (In rural areas, children are told that the spirit of the rice cries if it is not eaten up.)

(k) The host or hostess is always pleased if a guest asks for seconds; it is a sign of faith and trust (in rural areas) and of appreciation of the good food (in both rural and urban areas). A quiet belch after a meal is a sign of appreciation, but if you follow this custom, please do not overdo it!

(l) Taboo! Do not blow your nose, clear your throat loudly, or spit, while in the presence of other diners.

Dinner Parties

1   An invitation to a dinner party or celebration at a Malay home will be given in person, if at all possible. It is rude to refuse an invitation made by a personal call. Refusing a written invitation will not give as much offence.

2   A Malay may invite a friend to his house on "Saturday", at 1930 hours, but he might really mean that the guest should come on Friday at 1930 hours. Do not be confused by this. Malays consider the new day to begin at about 1830 hours. Thus "Saturday" really starts at about 1830 hours on Friday evening. It would be wise, however, to check with your host, so there will be no mistake!

3   Guests arrive on time, or about ten to fifteen minutes earlier. If they know their hosts quite well, it is good manners for women guests to offer to help in the preparations. In rural areas, friends and neighbours are expected to come early to help prepare the feast.

Restaurant Eating

It is not common for a Malay to entertain guests in a restaurant. The home is much preferred. The reason for this: if a Malay does not invite guests to his home it would be a slur on his wife—it would indirectly cast doubt on her cooking ability.

DATING AND COURTSHIP

In Singapore, some young people of working or university age mix with friends of their own age, but dating, according to the Western fashion, is not common. If a young man takes a girl out several times, her parents expect an engagement to be forthcoming. Most of the mixing between young people takes place in school, or in groups. The young people generally come from the same community, and are usually well known to the parents. Girls in a Malay community strive to protect a good reputation. Their future marriage depends on their good character, religious background and their standing in the community. Random dating endangers this position.

Malays still arrange marriages, but it is rare for a marriage of total strangers to take place. Previously, close family friends arranged engagements for their children when they were still infants (the marriage to take place when they came of age), but today young people have much more say in the choice of a marriage partner. Today, Malays are concerned that their marriages are based on affection and respect. While parents may still arrange marriages, young people must give their full mutual consent.

When an unmarried boy reaches 25-28 years, his parents start to drop broad hints like: "Don't you think it's time you were getting married?" If he agrees, but has not decided on a girl yet, his mother starts to make enquiries for a suitable partner. She is not above sending out some friends to visit the girl's family and to check up on the girl's cooking, manners, disposition, etc. However, this type of marriage is not so common today; it may only be used if the young people are very shy. It is more common for a young man to choose the girl first, then to go to his family for help in arranging the marriage. His mother, or one of her friends, approaches the girl's mother. Being very careful to make the suggestion as delicately as possible, she says something like "You have a beautiful cage in your home. I have a lonely bird. Can my bird stay in your cage peacefully?" The girl's mother usually takes one or two weeks to discuss it with her daughter and the family. If there is some problem, the girl's parents are very tactful in their refusal; there is no desire to hurt feelings or to cause loss of face. A negative answer will be given as gently as possible: "My daughter is very young, she is not yet ready for marriage."

MUSLIM MARRIAGE AND DIVORCE

In the old days, Malays often married cousins. It is a long-standing Malay custom that predates their conversion to Islam. There is nothing in Islam that forbids this custom. However, a Malay would not marry just any cousin—there were certain restrictions. For example, a marriage between the children of brothers was not preferred. It was thought that if a marriage of this kind should end in divorce, it might cause hard feelings between the brothers. There were also "generational" differences that prevented marriages between cousins. Thus, a Malay girl could marry the son of her parents' older siblings but not the son of their younger siblings. A Malay boy could marry the daughter of his parents' younger siblings but not the daughter of their older siblings. Today, this custom is dying out and Malays do not encourage their children to marry cousins because they feel that "the blood will be strengthened" by marrying out. They prefer a marriage with a fine young girl or boy from the same community. They would be especially pleased if the family were well known to them.

In the not-so-old days, marriage was seen primarily as an alliance between two families. The young couple formed a partnership based on contractual expectations. Romantic love and infatuation were thought of as unnecessary (and, indeed, even as a hindrance) to a marriage. They felt that if the young couple "fell out of love" the marriage would have nothing left to sustain it. Romantic love was seen as a form of temporary insanity. (Modern science seems to agree with this view. Psychologists agree that there must be more than infatuation to make a successful marriage; mutual trust, respect, affection, etc. are important!) If a man and his wife were too emotionally involved they were thought of as a bit strange, maybe even bewitched. Today, this concept has changed. Affection, love and respect are recognised as necessary to the maintenance of a stable relationship, hence young people have more say in the choice of a marriage partner.

Divorce was easily obtainable *by a man* several years ago. If there was conflict and disharmony in a relationship, the Muslim husband could formally divorce his wife by pronouncing *talak* ("I divorce thee") three times before reliable witnesses. (*Talak* can be pronounced in stages. The first is the one-*talak* divorce, where the man says *talak* only once; the couple is then separated but may be reconciled. Should trouble begin again, the man cannot resort to the one-*talak* divorce a second time; he must pronounce the two-*talak* divorce. Here, again, reconciliation is possible. The two-*talak* divorce can also be pronounced only once. The final step is the three-*talak* divorce. A woman who has been divorced by three *talaks* cannot remarry her husband until she has married and been divorced by another man.) Today, this is not true. Malays themselves are quick to point out the disadvantages of divorce, polygyny, and easy remarriage. Also, a woman can now file a complaint, and, in some cases, she can institute divorce proceedings if she has good reason to do so, e.g., sterility, adultery, or lack of maintenance. The Syariah Court now provides services to help with counselling and reconciliation. It discourages early marriage; it insists on full mutual consent between the boy and the girl; it does not grant divorce easily (where there are differences, it encourages the one-*talak* divorce); and it does not allow polygyny except in extreme cases, e.g. insanity or barrenness on the part of the wife.

Polygyny was, and still is, legal for Muslims. It is, however, a rare occurrence, perhaps because Malay women today are too independent to settle for this type of marriage. When polygyny was first affirmed by the Prophet, it was a humanitarian concern. It was intended to take in the widows and children of the men who had been killed in war—a form of social welfare.

ENGAGEMENT

Once a proposal has been accepted, the boy's family sends some elderly representatives (the father's brother or other relatives) to make the arrangements with the girl's family. The parents do not directly engage in negotiations as it is considered indelicate for them to talk face-to-face about financial matters. During this meeting, they decide on a date for the wedding, the bride-price (which helps to pay for the wedding expenses, about $1000 or so), and they bring gifts of fruit, cakes, clothing, jewellery and cosmetics. They give the girl a ring, and she gives them one for the boy in return.

The meeting is held in a specially decorated room, and the girl is dressed beautifully. The boy's delegation comes in to present the gifts to her and to feast their eyes on the future member of their family.

The date of the wedding is often set for a year or two in advance. During this time, she is allowed to date the boy, with restrictions. Decorum and propriety are expected from both of them. This extended time gives the young couple an opportunity to grow close to each other; it also allows the boy enough time to save the bride-price. The young man also gives a monthly gift of money to his fiancee, to show that he is assuming responsibility for his future bride. (His relatives helping to arrange the marriage will delicately hint to the boy's family: "Do not let your bird be hungry; it is better to have a little water and seed in the cage!") The sum is usually about $50. His fiancee normally saves this for her trousseau or for their future. In the old days (and in some rural areas today) the young girl was not allowed to see her fiancee during this period. She was closely chaperoned by her mother to emphasize her purity and modesty.

Malay parents do not like to see a girl marrying before her elder sisters do. If this happens, the young man must bring gifts to the older sisters in compensation "for stepping over the obstacle" (*langkah bendul*). They do not mind if the girl marries before her elder brothers do.

Etiquette at Engagements

A *kenduri* (feast) is given at the time of the engagement. Friends and family are invited. The *kenduri* for a wedding is called *walimah*. Gifts are not expected. Women usually wear long skirts and blouses (modest), the men wear casual clothes, no tie.

THE WEDDING

A Malay wedding is full of music, colour, excitement and splendour. It used to go on for days, but now, in urban areas, it ordinarily lasts only two days: usually Saturday (for the private ceremony, legalizing the marriage) and Sunday (for the public ceremony, the *bersanding*).

Before the ceremonies begin, the bride is attended to by a woman, called the "Mak Andam", who helps with the wedding protocol. The groom's family pays for her special skills. It is her duty to prepare the bride for the wedding. The Mak Andam performs certain rituals and beautifying ceremonies on the bride. She shaves the forehead, trims the eyebrows, and cuts off all the unruly hair from around the hairline; she may even file the front teeth. All this attention ensures that the bride has a fresh and radiant appearance. It also has another purpose! By observing the way the three strands of hair at the centre of the forehead fall after cutting, the Mak Andam is able to tell whether the girl is a maiden or not. If there is any doubt as to the bride's purity, the information is available to the couple's parents on request. The secret of this ritual has been handed down to Mak Andams through the generations. It is also the Mak Andam who provides the bride-to-be with instructions about the physical side of marriage. Unmarried girls are not allowed to be present when these instructions are being given. (Traditionally, the bride is expected to put up a show of resistance to her husband on their first night together. It shows that she is pure and modest, and that she has been brought up properly. The bride's mother could take comfort in the length of time her daughter took in avoiding her husband.) The Mak Andam then bathes the girl with water and limes to symbolically purify her.

On Saturday evening, the legal wedding ceremony takes place. It is called the *akad nikah*. The bride sits in the bridal chamber, which is decorated like a page out of the *Arabian Nights*. Silks, satins, sequins, fine curtains and canopies beautify the room. (Women love this part of the festivities; they can't wait to see how skilfully the family has adorned the room!) The groom waits in the hall with his relatives and friends. The Kathi (a man versed in Syariah law who is authorised to perform Muslim marriages) speaks to the bride and groom separately. They sign the marriage certificate.

After the signing, the groom pays a "marriage fee" (*mas kahwin*) to the bride. (The sum is optional, but in Singapore, $22.50 seems to be the usual sum. In the good old days, it was only $2.50. In Malaysia the fee differs from state to state.) The groom then *salams* with the bride. Long ago, if it was an arranged marriage, this would be the first time that the groom had seen or touched his bride. Even though they are now legally married, the couple do not "stay together" until after the *bersanding*.

Akad Nikah — the wedding is solemnized the night before the *bersanding.* The young man signs the registry papers required by the State, and the "bride-price" is also exchanged. *Photo: Times Publishing, Singapore*

Although the bride looks solemn, a Malay wedding is a time for happiness and gaiety. The bride must appear sober and with eyes downcast to show the state of her purity and modesty. *Photo: Straits Times, Singapore*

Mandi-mandi — watering ceremony. After two days of marriage, it is the Malay custom to have a public bath. This symbolizes the washing away of the carefree childhood days and represents the beginning of maturity. After the couple has been "bathed", all the family and friends join in on a public water-pouring ceremony. *Photo: Straits Times, Singapore*

The *bersanding* is held the following day. Guests begin arriving in the morning and festivities continue till late in the afternoon. As soon as the groom arrives at the house, the bride appears. While the groom bargains with the bride's male relatives to gain entry to the house, she takes her seat on the left side of the *pelamin* (a raised platform, something like a throne). The Mak Andam holds a fan before her face. When the groom is led to the *pelamin* he bargains with the Mak Andam to remove the fan so that he can see his bride's face. He then takes his seat on the *pelamin*. Both are splendidly dressed in bridal costumes (often rented from the Mak Andam). King and queen for the day, they hold court for all their friends and relatives. Some of the guests throw yellow rice over both shoulders of the couple to bless them and wish them good luck.

During these activities, the bride must keep her eyes downcast and assume a shy and modest appearance. She is not to laugh, smile or look around. This is the ideal behaviour expected of her. It indicates her state of modesty and purity. Her friends will try to tease her and cause a giggle or two with remarks like: "Be patient", "Happy landing", etc., but her face remains motionless. After an hour or so on their "throne" they step down. There is usually a repeat of the *bersanding* in the evening, sometimes with a Western-style feast as well. There is usually a modern band playing Western pop music in cities. In Malacca there is often Malay dancing and music at the wedding feast.

Guests are given a *bunga telur* to take home with them. It is a hard-boiled egg nestled in a basket, or glass, with some paper flowers.

Etiquette at Weddings

Gifts

1   A present for the kitchen is the most desirable gift a guest can bring. Traditionally, a bride must be able to set up a fully-equipped kitchen when she marries, so kitchen utensils, dishes, pots, teapots, wooden-spoon sets, serving dishes, fruit bowls and cake dishes make useful gifts. Do not give knives, ashtrays, wine glasses, or nightgowns.

2   Money can be given, but a personally-chosen gift is more appreciated. If money is given, it should be given discreetly. It is usually wadded up into a small packet and handed to the father of the bride or to his trusted friend (who acts as his representative) in the midst of a *salam*.

3   The present can be wrapped in traditional wedding paper, or red (symbol of love), or green (symbol of religion).

The Wedding Banquet

1   About a week before the wedding, it is traditional for the relatives and close friends to bring offerings of food to the bride's house. This is used in the preparation of the feast. Good gifts for a close friend of the family to give are: uncooked rice, onions, fruit, oil, live chickens, sugar, even firewood.

2   It is usually "open house" on the day of the wedding feast. People generally come between 1100 and 1700 hours. The *bersanding* is usually held around 1500 hours.

3   Men and women are seated separately, although the host will not object to Western men and women sitting together. If the feast is at night, men and women often sit together. It is a good idea to observe the local guests and to follow suit.

4   Guests eat with the fingers of the right hand. Westerners should be prepared to follow Malay custom, rather than add to the chores of the servers by asking for forks and spoons.

Dress

1   Women should wear modest clothes: no revealing, plunging necklines or backless, strapless gowns. A long skirt, or at least one that covers the knees, and a long-sleeved blouse is in good taste. Women usually take the opportunity to wear all their gold jewellery.

2   Men can dress casually, in sports shirts with open collars or batik shirts. Malay men usually wear their national dress, the *baju kurung.*

Behaviour

1   Have fun, but be restrained: no loud laughter, wild gestures, shrill voices, etc.

2   Ask for permission before taking photographs.

3   In cities, the bride's hand can be shaken by male guests.

In rural areas, only women shake the bride's hand. (Note: Malay men often shake hands or *salam* with the bride, but only if she has her hand in a glove.)

BIRTHS

A Malay baby is a lucky baby! He is born into a warm and loving community. His parents will rear him with considerable gentleness and tenderness. He will rarely be scolded or punished; instead, he will be taught through example and praise. There will be no lack of physical affection or cuddling for the child. Malays recognise the importance of close physical contact for babies, and fathers, mothers, siblings, and kin will make sure that the child has full emotional support and tender touching. Visitors to Malaysia will be impressed with the happy, playful and smiling children they see there.

Parents observe many restrictions while waiting for the birth of their baby: Women will not sew any seamed article in the belief that the child's anus will be closed at birth if they do so; a mother is careful not to expose herself to any experience which may cause shock or trauma for this may upset the unborn baby; a mother does not sleep in the afternoon between 1800 and 1900 hours (prayer time) in the belief that the child will be lazy if she does. The parents will not be cruel to any living creature in the belief that the child may suffer some deformity from this.

Today, many Malays go to the hospital to deliver their babies, but rural Malays prefer to have the child at home with the services of a midwife. The reasons for this are many, the most important one being that the father plays a crucial role in the rituals that are performed soon after birth:

1   As soon as his wife has given birth, the father washes the blood stains from the cloth that the mother has lain on during delivery. This is symbolic of the responsibility that he assumes as husband to his wife and father to his child.

2   The placenta is seen as a "twin" of the newborn baby.
    Soon after delivery, the father places the placenta in a
    clay pot with a cover. Some rock salt is added to the
    placenta in the pot. It is kept for forty days, then the
    father buries it under the house. The salt is a sign of
    friendship between the child and the father. The placenta
    is buried as if it were the "twin" who has "died".

3   Every child is seen to be a carrier of "light"; this light
    should be seen to burn firstly in his own home. The
    Malays also believe that the child's first cry should be
    heard in his own home as it is "a cry of loyalty to and
    respect for his parents". After the first cry, the father takes
    a clean white cloth that has been dipped in boiled water.
    He rubs the child's mouth to open it wide. This is a
    symbolic act to indicate that the child will always speak
    the truth. He then rubs the eyelids gently with his thumbs,
    starting from the inside and working towards the outer
    corners. This symbolizes that the child should see nothing
    but good in the world. Next the father softly sings or
    calls the Muslim prayer into his child's ear so the child
    will always remember the greatness of Allah. (He may
    also strike a stone pestle against a mortar, close to his
    child's ear to test the child's reflexes.)

These ritualized and symbolic acts make for a close bond
between father and child from the very first moments of the
child's life.

The Malay mother will never, if at all possible, use artificial
feeding for her baby. She believes that breast milk enters the
blood of the child and this cultivates a respect and closeness
that will last throughout life. In addition, she believes that the
milk strengthens the child's spirit as well as his body, that it
develops his faith and his character, that it makes a bond so
spiritual that nothing can destroy the relationship of the child
and his mother. The child may be breastfed until he is willing
to give up the practice himself. The child is often put to his
mother's breast in times of physical and emotional stress,

whether he is hungry or not, and whether his mother has milk or not. The Malays recognise the psychological needs that the child has for comfort and security. They know that the physical need for food is only part of the total needs of the child. In this respect, many Western cultures are only beginning to understand what the Malays have known instinctively for centuries.

The child is given a name within two weeks of his birth so that it can be placed on the birth certificate. Forty-four days after his birth, a religious ceremony is held at home and the child's name is formally bestowed on him. A large *kenduri* follows.

Etiquette
Mothers are not given gifts on the birth of a baby, but, for the baby, little outfits, dresses or blankets are appreciated. Do not give toy dogs. There is no taboo about the number or colour of gifts though cheerful bright or pastel colours are in good taste. Visits may be made anytime after the first day.

CIRCUMCISION

Infant girls are circumcized (clitoridectomy). This is a symbolic gesture and a religious obligation. A tiny piece of the skin of the clitoris is removed. (A Malay woman demonstrated this amount by rolling a minuscule piece of paper tissue and indicating the tip of it with her fingernail.) No feast is given, but some neighbours and relatives may come in for refreshments.

Young boys are usually circumcized when they reach puberty, although this operation can be undergone soon after birth or between eight and twelve years of age. Today, a Muslim doctor may come to the house to perform it, along with a *mudim*, a man who specializes in circumcision. In rural

The young boy is dressed almost like a miniature groom for his circumcision ceremony. His friends are dressed like Arabs — they show the Arab influence in this ritual. *Photo courtesy of Asiah Harun*

areas, several boys may have the operation together. Circumcision is a religious obligation for Muslims. The Malays consider it essential for personal health and hygiene. Anthropologists feel that it is a rite that celebrates the passage of the boy from childhood to young manhood.

The ceremony that goes hand in hand with the circumcision varies from place to place, but in rural areas it goes something like this: A large feast is held in the afternoon. Friends and relatives come to support and congratulate the boys (usually brothers and cousins go through the ceremony together). The boys are dressed in traditional Malay costume. They sit at the feast, but rarely have any appetite! At about 1500 hours, they bathe at the well, carefully cleaning the penis and foreskin. One boy may volunteer to go first. (It is said that he will be the first to marry!) He sits on a banana stem or stool while his father's friend sits behind to hearten and hold him. (Some of the young men I interviewed jokingly said that they were held like this so they wouldn't try to run away or climb a tree!) The *mudim* reassures the boy by quietly talking to him. The foreskin is stretched with a peg and is quickly cut off with a razor-sharp knife. Some medication is applied and the boy is bandaged and he is limpingly led away to a ceremonial mattress. Prior to this, he may only have slept on a sleeping mat. A *sarung* is strung tent-like from the ceiling to cover him. His wound is dressed every day and he is given a special diet of grilled fish and rice; the fish must be grilled over an open fire. In ten or twelve days he is completely healed and he rejoices that he has "passed the test" and taken his first step into the world of manhood!

Etiquette
The *kenduri* for circumcision ceremonies is usually on a grand scale and guests must observe the correct dress for weddings. Ordinarily, money is given to the boy to cheer him up. The amount depends on how well you know him. Ten or twenty dollars is about normal.

FUNERALS

Muslims must be buried within twelve hours, sooner if possible. When a Malay dies, a Bilal or Iman (a man from the community or mosque who knows how to deal with the rituals) is called to the house. In the meantime, the body is prepared by members of the family. The deceased's children or relatives wash the body and fold the arms over the chest, then cover it with a white cloth. The head would already have been placed in a position facing Mecca. Someone always stays with the body. Some chapters of the Koran are read. Muslims believe that the soul of the person lives on after death. It goes into the hands of Allah and remains there until the day of judgment.

When the Iman comes, he cleanses the body ritually—first with pure water, then with camphor water—to keep it from developing an odour. The body is wrapped in three layers of white cloth; the last layer will be arranged to look like clothes, but there will be no stitches in the material. Herbs are sprinkled over the body. Before the face is wrapped, the family comes in and the Iman says a few words. Prayers are said and the body is taken to the mosque or directly to the graveyard.

The coffin is not like a Western one; the body is laid on a plank and covered. (If the soil is damp at the graveyard, then a box-like coffin can be used.) The grave is cut into a depression adjacent to the actual pit. The body lies in the depression, on its right side with the face in the direction of Mecca. A plank covers the body so that no soil falls on it or surrounds it.

Muslims do not fear a natural death. They have a saying that goes: "When you think that tomorrow you will die, you will live forever." They do fear a disastrous death: accident, suicide, or murder. They feel that in these cases, they will not be able to fulfil the purpose in their lives and their duties to Allah and their family. A good Muslim prays for a peaceful death, one where he has had the opportunity to make his peace with Allah and say his prayers before dying.

Etiquette for Visitors
1 Friends and neighbours come to the house and they are allowed to see the face of the deceased for one "last look". Guests pay their respects by standing quietly while viewing the body, bowing the head and making a silent prayer.
2 There may be some light refreshments served—coffee or

tea with biscuits, sometimes food—but these will be served only before the ritual cleansing of the dead.

3   Muslims do not mourn visibly; they try to restrain their grief. There should be no loud talking or excessive noise. Weeping and wailing will not be seen in public.

4   *Gifts:* Flowers can be sent to the home. Money is often given to the family. It is brought in a white envelope and handed to the mourners. Any amount is acceptable and depends on how well you know the deceased's family, but $10 or $20 is usually given.

5   *Clothes:* White is traditional for funerals but sombre colours are acceptable.

5 The Indian Community

THE PEOPLE

Seven per cent of the people of Singapore and eleven per cent of the people of Malaysia are Indians.

"How would you describe the typical Indian?" I asked my Indian friend. She answered, "Well, we have knobby knees, skinny calves, our arms are the same size at the bottom as they are at the top, our men have pot bellies, and our women have at least three rolls of fat between the top of the sari and the bottom of the *choli* (little blouse worn with a sari); but we have high cheek bones, even white teeth, large dark eyes and luxuriant black hair." I feel that she has overestimated the negative and underestimated the positive. Indians are a physically beautiful people. They have a lively sense of humour, and their personalities are generally warm and vibrant.

The Indians of Singapore and Malaysia come from many

parts of India and belong to many faiths. Most of them are Hindus, but there are a large number of Indian Muslims and Sikhs. They are to be found in every strata of the class structure: there are Indian doctors and lawyers, trade unionists, police and army personnel, small stall-keepers and labourers. They range from the modern and the liberal to the conservative and traditional.

Singapore Indians who are of the Muslim religion own most of the shops in and around Arab Street. Indian Muslims can also be found in their textile shops in Jalan Tuanku Abdul Rahman in Kuala Lumpur. Many of them have families in India. They come here and lead a bachelor-like existence while sending money home to their families. They usually sell textiles, perfumes, and jewellery. They are pleasant salesmen; a tourist can stop and pass the time of day with them for hours —they don't seem to mind if a customer browses around and doesn't buy anything. The perfume man will mix special exotic fragrances for you alone. He can blend a perfume that will capture the heart of any man! He will let you sniff every perfume in the shop, show you the most expensive oils in the world, and will not even be disappointed if you buy only one or two small samples to try out at home. He may even give you a goat-skin flask as a remembrance!

Indians of different sects and religions observe different customs; thus it is very difficult to speak of a universal pattern of manners and etiquette for the Indian community. The majority of the Indians in Singapore and Malaysia come from Southern India and are Tamils, so most of the habits and customs in this chapter will be Tamil ones.

To get the "feel" of the Indian community, one should visit Serangoon Road in Singapore or Jalan Brickfields in Kuala Lumpur. Most of the local Indians do their shopping there: saris, slippers, men's *dhotis,* heavy steel cooking utensils, brass stands and lamps for prayer, spices, herbal medicines, betel nuts, jewellery, etc. can be found in the small shops that line

An Indian shop on Serangoon Road. Notice the tray of betel leaves in the foreground. Indians love to chew on these after meals, wrapped around some white lime paste, a kind of red bark paste and some chopped betel nuts. Flower garlands hang further down the five-foot way. Note carefully the use of the right hand only when exchanging money, goods or small objects. *Photo: JoAnn Craig*

these streets. Also along Serangoon Road and Jalan Brick-fields are many little flower stands which sell garlands for weddings and scented fresh flowers for the family altar. It is the custom for Indian women to wear flowers in their hair to celebrate joy in their marriage, to enhance their beauty, and to complement their beautiful saris. A husband often stops on his way home from work to buy a flower for his wife's hair. An Indian woman is happiest when she has bright bangles on her arms, flowers in her hair, and is secure in the knowledge that her husband finds her lovely. If the husband of an Indian woman dies, she will never again wear flowers in her hair or bangles on her arms.

Indians have a deep faith which is woven into their

everyday lives. Every morning, before the sun is up, the Indian mother offers prayers and burns incense at the family altar to greet her god and the new day. She may do this at sunset too. Friday is a special day. Indians flock to temples to offer prayers. They make several different kinds of offerings. A "banana" offering or a "half-coconut" offering is the most typical. For a donation of 30 cents (for a banana) or 80 cents (for half a coconut), they write down their name on a small slip of paper and the priest reads out the name during the formal prayers. The blessed fruit (banana or coconut) is taken home and can be eaten or placed on the family altar. They are given holy ash to put on their foreheads and betel nuts that can be chewed by the older folks, or else placed on the altar. If the offerings are not eaten, they will not be thrown away after they have become rotten. Instead, they will be placed under a tree, or into a river.

You often see an Indian woman with a red dot on her forehead: it is a symbol of her marriage. (A North Indian woman wears a red streak on the parting of her hair.) An unmarried woman sometimes wears a black dot on her forehead. This black colour is used to counteract the effect of the evil eye! If a young girl gets too many compliments, Indians feel that some kind of harm may come to her and this dot is supposed to repel evil influences. Modern young girls match the dots on their foreheads with the colour of their saris. This is not traditional, only fashionable. Older people may shake their heads over this practice.

THAIPUSAM

To understand the heart of the Indian, one must understand his Hinduism! An example of his faith can be seen in the Thaipusam festival in Singapore and Malaysia. This festival is celebrated in these countries on an even more elaborate scale than it is celebrated in its own homeland, South India.

(In India, the Government forbids the use of spikes and spears for penetrating the body.)

Thai- (meaning month of January-February) *pusam* (meaning festival) usually takes place in late January or early February. The entire Indian community turns out for the celebration. According to R. Raj Kumar, a student of the University of Singapore, who has done research on this phenomenon, the rituals in Thaipusam enhance the social identity of the community. Thaipusam reinforces the spirit of "communitas" which means that, on this day, every Indian is equal in the sight of every other Indian. Women have equal status with men; lower castes have equal status with higher castes; and there is no distinction made between individuals. Thaipusam also adds to the solidarity of the Indian community as it enhances their sense of "Indianness", which is very important in multi-ethnic cultures such as Singapore and Malaysia.

In Singapore, most of the activity takes place in Serangoon Road, the heart of the Indian community! In Malaysia, most of the proceedings take place along the banks of the Gombak River near the Batu Caves. The Indians in Malaysia who take part in this festival bathe in the river to purify themselves before preparing to bear the *kavadis* up the 272 steps to the shrine of Murugan, in the Batu Caves. The Malaysian Indians climb the steps because of the Hindu myth that says "one must climb up to worship" the Lord Murugan. The story is told: "Once upon a time, there was a god, Narada, who wanted to test the two sons of Siva, Vinayagar and Murugan. He said that he would give a golden apple to the first of them who could go around the world. Impetuous Lord Murugan, young and brave, quickly climbed on his peacock and flew off. Vinayagar, older and wiser, stopped for a few minutes and thought first. He asked Narada if there was any difference between the world and one's parents. Narada said, 'Of course not!' Vinayagar then walked around his parents three times, saying: 'My parents are my world and I go around them!'

Pleased with Vinayagar's response, Narada gave him the golden apple. When Murugan got back, all hot and tired and worn out from flying around the world, he was pretty cross to find out that Vinayagar had already received the golden apple. He flew off to the top of a hill called Palam-ne, and refused to come down. Those who wanted to worship him had to 'climb up to do so'." That's why all Lord Murugan's temples are built up on a high hill; except in Singapore where there are very few high hills!

Lord Murugan, who is venerated on Thaipusam day, represents virtue, bravery, youth and power. Indians carry a *kavadi* to him because of this myth: "Once upon a time there was a wise man, Agastiyar, who wanted two mountain peaks to meditate on. He sent his disciple to fetch them from the land where Lord Siva lived. The disciple went and picked up the two peaks, and placed them on his shoulders. Now, Lord Murugan, the son of Siva, wanted these peaks for himself. He thought of a way to trick the disciple into giving them to him. He took the form of a king, and went to find the disciple. When he found him he said: 'You look so tired, why don't you lie down and rest for a while?' While the disciple was sleeping, Lord Murugan took the form of a little boy and stood on the mountain peaks. When the disciple woke up he tried to lift the mountain peaks, but found that they were too heavy. He began to argue with the 'little boy', not realizing that he was the Lord Murugan. During the argument the disciple fell off the mountain and became unconscious. Meantime, after meditating and waiting for some time, the wise man went to look for his disciple, and when he found him, begged Lord Murugan to have mercy on them. Lord Murugan took pity on the disciple, and made him his guard. He then said that anyone who came to him bearing a *kavadi* would be blessed."

Today, Indians who wish to thank Lord Murugan for a favour granted, or to ask him for a petition, or even to make up for some deed, vow to carry a *kavadi* on their shoulders. This is done as a sacrifice, and the *kavadi* is seen as a sort of a

Faith helps this young Indian woman remain calm and composed as a silver *vel* pierces her cheek. The man doing the piercing and the onlookers seem to feel the pain more than she does. *Photo: New Nation, Singapore*

demi-chariot where the devotee carries the God upon his shoulders. (A *kavadi* can be any offering whatsoever, carried on the shoulders. There are many different kinds of *kavadi*.) The most common of all is the *Alavvu Kavadi*. It is a large semi-circular object, rather like half of a bicycle wheel. It is really a simple structure, but the Indians decorate it lavishly. Some Indians even have flashing lights intertwined among the peacock feathers and flowers that adorn the *kavadi*. *Kavadis* can be very heavy; some weigh up to 13–18 kilograms. Metal hooks or spikes attached to the *kavadi* are fastened onto the Indian's skin, or through it. Devotees may also pierce the tongue and/or cheeks with a small silver *vel*. The *vel* is shaped like a spear. The head of it is in the form

This man's skin is pierced with small pots containing milk. He is already in a trance as his friends help to prepare him for the *kavadi*. Metal hooks or spikes will be attached to the skin before the *kavadi* is lifted onto his shoulders. *Photo: Joe Craig*

of a heart and denotes purity of heart. The shaft symbolizes closeness to God. Overall, it is a symbol of victory over evil and of bravery and purity. Hindu mythology states that the *vel* was given to Murugan by his mother, Sakthi Devi, and it can always be seen in his hands. Contrary to what many people believe about Hinduism, *it is not a polytheistic religion.* Hindus believe in one Universal Spirit, without beginning or end, called Brahma (meaning World-Soul). This World-Soul is a Triune God. He is called the Three-in-One God, because Indians believe that God has different forms: Brahma is the Creator, Vishnu is the Preserver and Shiva is the Destroyer. They are not separate; they are only different aspects of the same divine Unity. Other attributes of the Triune God are symbolized by different "gods", i.e., Murugan symbolizes youth, bravery, virtue and power, but he is not believed to be a "god", instead, he is considered to be a reflection of some of the attributes of God.

The Indians who go through this ceremony are not mystics or holy men. They are just normal, average, everyday Indians—the student, the working man, the executive and the housewife. However, women do not carry the spiked *kavadi* as they are not allowed to bare their bodies in order to be pierced.

There are strict rules that the devotee must follow in order to purify himself before carrying the *kavadi*. He fasts from meat, fish and chicken, and he abstains from worldly pleasures, like sex, smoking and alcohol. The minimum period is three days, but the normal time is from one to two weeks before the festival.

These Indians may not know how to practise self-hypnosis, but they often meditate. Most important, they have a deep faith that permeates their everyday lives. At this festival, they go into a trance, ordinarily feel no pain and, oddly enough, rarely bleed or scar. Some Indians carry the *kavadi* for one Thaipusam; others vow to carry it on Thaipusam for three, five or seven years in succession. Some vow to carry it for life. In Singapore the devotees bear the *kavadi* from Perumal Temple in Serangoon Road to the Chettiar Temple in Tank Road, about four kilometres. Once inside the Chettiar Temple, they walk around the inside of the temple three times before placing the *kavadi* in front of the shrine of Lord Murugan. In Malaysia, the devotees have to climb the 272 steps that lead to the shrine of Lord Murugan. They do not complete their vow until they have placed the *kavadi* before the feet of Lord Murugan.

While the *kavadi* is being carried, the devotees walk the entire distance barefoot; several times along the way, people come out to wash the feet of the bearers. Friends, relatives and even strangers encourage and support the bearers by accompanying them every step of the way. They sing, dance, play music, and chant *"Vel, Vel, Vel"*. Limes are cut at strategic points along the way to ward off evil influences. After the hooks and spikes are removed from the skin of the *kavadi* bearer, "holy ash" is quickly rubbed into the wounds.

To understand the Hindu, one must understand his deep faith and his belief in the one Universal World-Soul. To witness this festival is a mystifying and exhilarating experience. Westerners have to understand the symbolism of the rituals in order to appreciate them.

LEARNING TO SOCIALIZE

Introductions

1   Indian men shake hands with each other. Some Indians, among themselves, especially younger people with older people, may use the traditional Indian greeting, with palms together in the prayer position, hands raised to the front of their face, and head bowed slightly. Traditionally, they do not shake hands with women.

2   Women may shake hands with each other, but usually not with men. They often use the traditional palms-together greeting when introduced. A North Indian woman might cover her head with the end of her sari before making the gesture.

3   In a Westernized setting, Indian men and women often conform to the Western style of handshaking between the sexes. Western women can use the traditional Indian form of greeting or just nod their heads and smile when introduced to an Indian gentleman.

4   The Western practice of saying the name of the older before the younger, the more important before the less important and the lady before the gentleman is still acceptable.

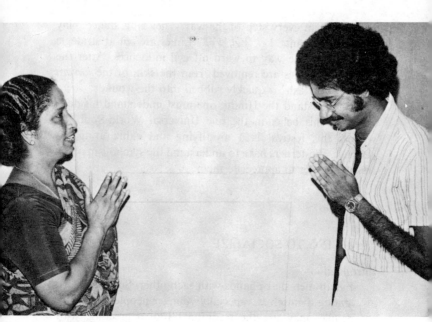

In modern Singapore and Malaysia, many young people do not use the traditional Indian greeting among their own peer group; however, the polite young person will always use it when greeting an older person. Notice the "social distance" between the two above? *Photo: JoAnn Craig*

Greetings

Western greetings are acceptable. If meeting an Indian friend around mealtime, Indians usually ask if he has eaten yet. The polite person answers in the affirmative.

Names: Hindus

1   Most Indians in Singapore and Malaysia trace their descent through their fathers. However, some Malayalee Indians are matrilineal, i.e. they trace their descent through their mothers and even inherit from them, e.g. the "Nairs".

2   The majority of Singaporean and Malaysian Indians do not have surnames. They use the initial of their father's name, placed before their own name. Let us take an example, M. Thiruselvam: "M" is the initial of the individual's father's name (say, Manickavasagam). Thiruselvam is the individual's own name. For the convenience of those with inflexible tongues, the name may be shortened to "Thiru" or "Selvam". Friends would call him Thiru, and business associates would call him Mr Thiru. The individual would normally choose whether to be known by the first or the last part of his name.

3   An Indian woman would normally drop her father's initial and use her husband's own name (not his initial) when she marries. So if a Miss T. Kamala marries M. Thiruselvam, she would be known formally as Mrs Thiruselvam, and casually as Kamala.

4   Some modern Indians have dropped this custom of adding initials to their names and have adopted surnames.

Names: Sikhs

Indians of the Sikh faith are recognized by their distinguished physique and their turbans. They have traditionally been regarded as warriors. Their religion is a blend of Hinduism and Islam and they are not supposed to adhere to a class or caste system. They trace their descent through their fathers but identify themselves in a different way from the South Indians.

1   An example of a Sikh man's name is Bhopinder Singh s/o Joginder Singh. Bhopinder is the individual's name. His friends call him Bhopinder and his business acquaintances call him Mr Bhopinder Singh. Singh is not a surname; it is a name given to all Sikh men to signify their brotherhood. Joginder Singh is Bhopinder's father's name and since Sikhs have no surname, they have the "son of" (s/o)

Warriors of the past, the Sikhs of today are peaceful people. This Sikh runs a restaurant where good fun and good talk are on the menu every day. *Photo: JoAnn Craig*

or "daughter of" (d/o) to indicate their parentage.

2   An example of a Sikh woman's name is Kamaljeet Kaur d/o Gurdev Singh, married to Bhopinder Singh. She would be known to her friends as Kamaljeet. Westerners would call her Mrs Bhopinder Singh. Kaur is the name given to all Sikh women and it is not a surname. Gurdev Singh is her father's name.

3   A modern trend among the Sikhs is to include a third

name as a surname. This is usually a name which tells the other Sikhs which village or clan the family originally came from. Hence, if Bhopinder Singh comes from the Gil clan, he may call himself Bhopinder Singh Gil or shorten it to B.S. Gil. His wife would then be Mrs. B.S. Gil.

SOME COMMON COURTESIES AND CUSTOMS

As Indian Muslims in Singapore and Malaysia observe the same general rules as Muslims the world over, many of their customs pertaining to religion will be the same as those found in the Malay section. Find out if your Indian friend is a Muslim before you offer him pork or before you let your dog loose around him. The name is a sure giveaway: an Indian Muslim would have a Malay-sounding name with a *bin* or *binti* for *son of* or *daughter of* (refer to Malay section: Names). The customs discussed here are, generally speaking, Hindu customs.

Books
Books are almost sacred to the Indians. They would never sit on a book or throw it about, or generally handle it in a disrespectful manner. This feeling for books probably began years ago when holy books were the only printed works in existence. Also, books are visible symbols of knowledge and learning—priceless possessions in the East. The Chinese also have this reverence for all books.

Clothes
When attending an Indian affair, or when visiting an Indian home, erotic zones must be covered. Modest dress is always in good taste and clothes intended to attract attention should be avoided. So, no shorts, mini-skirts, plunging, strapless, backless or braless dresses!

Gestures and Touching

1   Do not point at a person with the right or left forefinger, or with two fingers. You can gesture towards a person using the whole right hand, palm facing upwards. Do not call a person to you with a waggling finger. Indians beckon someone with the whole hand, palm facing downwards; the hand makes nearly a complete circle.

2   Do not pat a Hindu child on the head. Most Indians, even grown-ups, do not like to be touched on the head. They believe that the head is the most sensitive part of the body and that no chance should be taken to hurt it, even by touching or patting it.

3   Avoid casual touching of the opposite sex. Men can touch other men, and women can touch other women, but men and women should not touch each other. A public decorum must be shown when in public. Westerners should be careful of this when in restaurants, nightclubs, shops, etc. Do not demonstrate public affection (kissing, hugging, hand-holding, etc.) in an Indian community or social gathering.

4   Indian usually maintain a "social distance" with members of the opposite sex (about an arm's length away). The older generation respects this "body buffer zone" more than the younger generation does. If you observe a step backward when you stand too close to an Indian acquaintance, it probably does not mean that you have bad breath or body odour: it may only mean that you have invaded his body buffer zone.

5   When speaking with Indian friends, you may notice a certain kind of gesture with the head. They toss it quickly from side to side as only Indians can. It means consent or agreement. It is different from the Western shake of the head which means "no", but is close enough for one to be confused by it. Misunderstandings can arise if one misreads this gesture.

Right Hand

Indians do not use the left hand for social purposes—ever! (It is used for cleaning after using the toilet.) Be careful when handing gifts, food, money in shops, etc. Do not receive change, merchandise, etc. from an Indian shopkeeper with the left hand! (Of course, if you are handing a heavy object with the right hand, then the left hand can help.)

Shopping

1 As for the Chinese, it is thought to be a good omen for the rest of the day if the first customer of the day buys something, however small, and a bad omen if he leaves without making a single purchase. However, it is not as strong a superstition among Indians as among Chinese.

2 Money and merchandise should be handled with the right hand.

3 Do not touch a clerk of the opposite sex.

Smoking

1 Do not offer an Indian woman a cigarette. Most of them do not smoke.

2 Ask for permission to smoke in an Indian home. In the presence of elderly Indians it is better to refrain from smoking.

3 Indians, even adult Indians, do not smoke before their parents. It is a gesture of respect.

4 Sikhs may not allow smoking in their homes at all for smoking is prohibited in their religion.

Temples

1 Shoes should always be removed before entering a temple. Leave them to the right or left side of the door so as not to block the doorway with them.

2 Indians step over the threshold, not on it!

3 Indians ordinarily bathe before going to the temple. Once they are there, they wash their feet, face and eyes before

Passage to the *Sanctum Sanctorum.* The screen, placed at the entrance, is removed just before daily worship. Only priests are allowed to enter this place. Visitors to the temple should not go further than the steps in front of the screen. Inset shows the main deity of this temple, Lord Vinayagar.

entering. To be really polite, the Westerner can wash his feet before entering.

4 Statues or religious pictures inside the temple must not be touched.

5 It is permissible to speak quietly and wander around, but keep silent if there are services going on.

6 Do not enter or walk into the *Sanctum Sanctorum.* It is usually the place where the statues of the deities are kept.

7 Women (even Western women) must not enter a temple when they are menstruating.
8 Women can wear pantsuits, slacks, etc. Ideally, legs should be covered (at least over the knee). Wear modest dress. Men do not wear hats in the temple.
9 Ask for permission before taking photographs.
10 If you ask a priest for a prayer, leave an offering of a dollar or two.

VISITING AN INDIAN HOME

Invitations
1 An Indian will extend an invitation to a dinner, etc., as informally as possible, and, unless it is a formal affair, like a wedding, a telephone call or a personal call is much preferred to a written note.
2 If an Indian friend invites you to "come over in the evening", this can mean anytime after 1600 hours. It would be advisable to arrange a specific time with your friend.
3 An Indian would prefer an invitation which includes a definite time and place. Do not say vaguely, "Drop in sometimes"; it is better to say, "Can you come over for coffee tomorrow morning at about 10.30?"
4 Indians also prefer an invitation to state specifically who is invited: the couple, the children, or the whole family!
5 Indians are usually punctual for invitations and appointments, so guests should also strive to be neither too early nor too late. (Note: Close Indian friends sometimes operate on "Indian Standard Time", which can mean anything from an hour or so around the specified time.)

Shoes
1 Many Indians do not wear shoes in the house. They are usually left at the door, to the right or left, or in a special

place for them near the door. Some Westernized Indian homes may not follow this custom, so see whether the members of the family wear shoes, and follow suit.

2   Even if the family wears shoes in the house, they will never ordinarily wear them in the kitchen for some Indian women sit and prepare food on the floor. Shoes are not worn then for hygienic reasons. A guest would not normally go into a kitchen though.

3   In many traditional Indian homes there is an area set aside for prayer, a *pooja* (prayer) room. Statues or pictures of Hindu deities will be found here. Shoes *must never be worn* in a house that has a *pooja* room. Indians believe that shoes must always be removed where prayers are said.

General

1   Women guests should be modestly dressed when visiting an Indian home.

2   Guests can bring some fruit or sweets for the children if they know the family fairly well.

3   Guests are ordinarily entertained in the living room and should not wander about or peer into other rooms of the house, unless invited to do so.

Sitting

1   Guests are invited to be seated. Wait until asked, then sit where the host indicates a place for you.

2   Seating is usually on chairs, but if they are not provided, as for funerals, weddings, etc., guests can sit cross-legged (men) or with knees together to the left or right (women) on the mats provided for such occasions.

3   In the presence of elders, do not cross one leg over the other or drape yourself over the sofa. Always show respect for them: rise, or at least half-rise from your chair when an older person enters the room for the first time. Even adults are highly respectful of elders. One Indian

man says: "When my father comes in, my crossed leg automatically comes down."

Conversation

1   Conversation between men and women is generally kept to a minimum. If women are present, men should be careful in their speech—no risque jokes or sex talk.
2   Also avoid discussions about politics and religion. Indians will discuss religion if the guest is sincere, but it is in bad taste to "argue religion".

Segregation of the Sexes

1   In many *traditional* Indian homes, the wife does not sit down when male guests are present. She may serve them, but otherwise she will stay in the kitchen or in some other part of the house.
2   When men and women guests are present at the same time, it is normal to see the women sitting together in one part of the room or house and the men in another part of the room or house.
3   Some modern or Westernized Indians have discarded this practice. Even traditional Indians put aside this custom out of courtesy when they have Western guests, but if the guests see this kind of segregation, it is good manners to follow the family's customs.

On Being a House Guest

1   Many allowances will be made for a Western guest in an Indian home. The Indian host will be mostly concerned that the guest make himself one of the family. Guests should observe the family etiquette and try to fit into their routine. If the family does not wear shoes in the home, then follow suit. The Indian host loves a guest who is adaptable, flexible and good-humoured. Eat heartily! The hostess will be pleased if she knows that you are a "good eater".

2   A woman guest can ask the hostess if she can help with the household chores in some way.

3   It is not considered presumptuous to do things on your own, but polite guests should inform the family of plans to go shopping, have lunch out, etc.

4   When a member of an Indian family leaves the house, for any purpose, the others do not say "goodbye": it is a bad omen. They say "Go and come back". The person leaving says "I'm going and I'll come back." If this exchange is not given, they feel that something unfortunate may happen. It is a good idea to follow this custom while staying in an Indian home.

5   Indians do not call a person back into the house once they have gone out of the door. If they must go back into the house for something they have forgotten, they must sit down and have a drink of water, etc., and then prepare to leave all over again, as if for the first time. They feel that it is a bad omen not to observe this custom.

6   Three people will not leave the house at the same time. Two will go out, and the third will follow later. They feel that the venture will not be successful otherwise.

7   *Bathroom Facilities:* In Singapore and Malaysia, some Indians have a standard-type shower. Others will have a tap and a bucket. In traditional homes the person stands and rubs oil over the body and hair; he scrubs with a special scrubber made from a plant; then soap is applied. All this is washed off with water from the shower or the bucket. The beauty-conscious may be interested in the ritual that Indian women go through before bathing: they apply a paste of a special flour and water to the hair and skin. It is said to keep the skin young-looking and soft to the touch. (Observe any Indian woman's skin and you will see the truth in this!)

8   The type of toilet you find will depend on the home you visit, but many have the squat-type toilet. Toilet paper

may be provided for guests, but usually a bucket of water and the left hand is used for cleansing.

Bread-and-butter Gifts

Among themselves, Indians do not give bread-and-butter gifts. They would wish to return the hospitality at some future time. But since Westerners may not have the opportunity to return hospitality, it is a nice gesture to give some lovely gift for the house: a pretty serving dish filled with sweets, a bowl of fruit, some beautiful sari material, etc. If there are children in the house, it is a good idea to bring a gift for the children. In any case, a thank you note after the visit is always appreciated.

Gifts in General

1 Indians do not open gifts in front of the guest. It is good manners to set them aside until after the guest has gone.

2 At certain times of the year, such as Deepavali, gifts like fruit and sweets may be set on the altar.

3 A gift may be reciprocated by an invitation to dinner or a return gift.

4 Colours to avoid are white and black. Red, yellow, green and all bright colours are happy colours for the Indians.

5 Odd numbers are usual when money is given as a gift. A dollar is usually added to the amount to make it uneven, and lucky: $11.00, $21.00, etc.

6 Do not ever give frangipanni. These are fragrant blossoms that look like bridal bouquets. They grow on trees in clusters and are very common in Singapore and Malaysia. These flowers are often made up into wreaths and sent to funerals. (These flowers are known as *Plumeria* to the Hawaiians who traditionally make leis from them.)

7 Do not give cigarettes or ashtrays to Sikhs. Liquor as a gift should also be avoided unless you personally know that the men of the house drink it.

8 Always offer a gift to an Indian with the right hand. Use the left hand to support the right hand.

FOOD AND DRINK

The restrictions mentioned here would apply only to Sikhs and Hindus. For the religious food customs of Indian Muslims, look under "Food and Drink" in the chapter on Malays.

1 Most Indians do not eat beef as the animal is venerated in their religion. The cow is considered to be a sacred animal because people consume its milk. The Indians feel that this is analogous to a human mother who gives milk.

2 Many Indians do not eat meat on Fridays.

3 Some Indians are vegetarians. Before you invite Indians to your home for a meal, it is a good idea to ask them if they are vegetarians.

4 Indians love spicy food, so a bottle of hot chilli sauce on the table is appreciated by Indian dinner guests. It's no use preparing delicately herbed dishes and subtle sauces for your Indian friends: they will murmur something about the "blandness" of the food while they pour hot chilli sauce over everything!

5 Colours are important: red (chilli), brown (curries) and yellow (turmeric) enhance the appearance of their food. Pungent aromas are the most enticing part of the meal. The rich colours and spicy fragrance of Indian dishes help to develop a great appetite!

6 Indians tend to like everything, including vegetables, well cooked. That is probably why salads are not too common at their meals. Singaporeans and Malaysians are becoming used to them but Indians from India usually do not favour raw vegetables.

7 Northern Indians love lentils *(dahl)* and wholewheat breads *(chapatis,* etc.). Wholewheat products form a staple part of their diet. Southern Indians, on the other hand, love rice. They don't feel that they have had a proper meal without it.

8 Indians are fond of yoghurt. A favourite yoghurt drink is

made by blending some plain yoghurt with a little water and crushed ice; salt or sugar can be added. (Southern Indians usually prefer salt, Northern Indians sugar.) They generally enjoy very sweet and rich desserts and butter, which they associate with nutrition. They generally do not enjoy: European cheeses with strong flavours, clams and other shellfish, boiled, steamed or bland foods.

9   They are not too familiar with Western wines, but many modern Indians enjoy wine once they have cultivated a taste for it. Indian women do not usually take alcoholic drinks.

Table Etiquette

1   *The Table Setting*
   (a) Serving bowls of food are usually placed in the centre of the table.
   (b) Plates are commonly placed on the table as in the Western manner.
   (c) Meals are sometimes served on banana leaves.
   (d) Forks and spoons are available for Western guests.
   (e) Knives will not be set on the table as the food will all be prepared in small bite-sized pieces.

2   *Seating*
   (a) Informality is the key note. There is generally no special place of honour, but the father of the family usually sits at the head of the table.
   (b) The host will generally invite the guests to sit where they wish. He may place a guest next to him or opposite him.
   (c) Men and women generally do not sit and eat together. The women normally serve the men first, then eat when the men are finished. For Western guests, an exception may be made. At informal functions, if there is a buffet-style meal, the women generally serve themselves first, then the men do the same. At these meals, seating may be mixed.

3   *Serving and Eating*

(a)   Hands should be washed before the meal.

(b)   Indians traditionally eat with the fingers of the right hand. The left hand must not be used for eating. It can be used to serve or pass dishes or to hold a glass if the right hand is soiled with food.

(c)   Guests may eat with the right hand if they wish, or use a fork and a spoon if they feel more comfortable with them. (Note: At celebrations, wedding receptions, etc., it is good manners to use the hands for eating if everyone else is doing so, rather than to ask for a fork and a spoon which may not be readily available. Guests usually feel more at ease if they eat the way everyone else does.)

(d)   Some Indians press and roll the food into a tidy bundle, then neatly convey it to their mouth by turning the hand upwards. They are careful not to drop any food onto the dish or table. Some are very adept at "flicking" the food into the mouth without dropping a grain. This is more difficult than it looks!

(e)   Fingers should not be sucked or licked. Do not soil the fingers of the hand above the second knuckle.

(f)   The guest should wait for the host to begin. The host generally picks up a serving dish and hands it to the guest to serve himself with, or he may serve the guest himself. He usually serves himself last.

(g)   The person serving is careful to put the food on the plate without touching the plate with the serving spoon.

(h)   Indians love to see a guest eat heartily. Second and third helpings are not unusual; a hostess will not be pleased with a "picky" eater.

(i)   Sometimes meals are served on banana leaves. The leaf is generally square-cut, and larger than a normal place-mat. A variety of sauces and curries are placed around a mound of rice. The leaf is larger

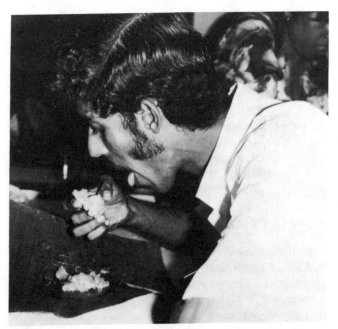

Eating with the hand is not a haphazard affair! The devout Hindu will quietly set aside a small portion of food as a thanksgiving offering to his God before beginning to eat. The fingers are never soiled above the second knuckle and the tongue sticks out slightly to receive the food which the thumb gently pushes into the mouth. *Photo: JoAnn Craig*

than necessary to give the eater plenty of elbow room at the table. At the end of the meal, the leaf is folded in half. Most Indians I observed fold the leaf in half away from the body. Other Indians say that it is a sign of appreciation for the "good" food to fold the leaf *towards* the body!

(j) Elbows should not be placed on the table in an upright position, as if to hold up the head. The elbow of the left hand can be rested on the table, with the hand dropped out of sight, towards the lap.

(k) The practice of taking tidbits from a husband's or wife's plate is not done in an Indian home.

(l) After the meal, forks and spoons, if used, can be placed on the dinner plate. There is no special manner of placing them. Indians wash their hands and often rinse out their mouths with tap water as well.

(m) Guests do not leave the table until the others have finished eating. After dinner, guests do not leave the home immediately. They usually sit and talk for some time in the living room.

PUBERTY CELEBRATIONS

Some Indians celebrate their daughters' "coming of age". The Sri Lankan Tamils have a ritual called *Chamathi Chadanja*. It is usually carried out at the time of the girl's first menses, but in Singapore or Malaysia it may be done just before the girl marries. The ceremony is carried out on an odd-numbered date, i.e., the seventh, ninth or eleventh day of the month.

The girl wears a new sari that has no black colour in it, black being the colour associated with evil. She is brought to sit among her relatives. Three women, usually happily married with children, attend her. They symbolize a happily-married life for the girl. One of these attendants would be the wife of the girl's mother's brother. (Her son is often the preferred marriage partner!) Some twigs, mud and dead leaves are placed at her feet to represent the dirt which will be washed away as a symbol of purification. In each hand she holds a little bundle containing a 10-cent coin and an areca nut wrapped in a betel leaf.

The girl's maternal uncle holds a pail of milk with coins and fine grass in it. The milk symbolizes purity, the coins are a symbol of wealth and the grass is a symbol of fertility. He pours a little of the milk on her head. Her three attendants

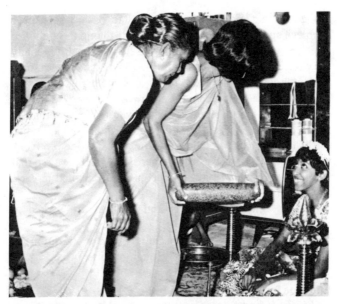

A young girl "comes of age". During the puberty ritual, the girl's aunts circle her three times with many symbolic objects. In this picture, the object is a grinding stone—symbol of a wife's fidelity. The story goes that a woman who was unfaithful to her husband was turned into a stone like the one in the photo. *Photo courtesy of Jayarani Pavadarayan*

and some other relatives (an odd number in all) also pour a bit of milk on her head. Her uncle then breaks a coconut into two halves: if it breaks cleanly, with no jagged edges, then it is believed that the girl has a happy marriage in store for her.

An odd number of married ladies, usually nine or eleven, carry trays to the three women attending the girl. These trays are passed in a circular motion around the girl, starting with her right side and over the right shoulder. Among the many symbolic items on the trays are a bamboo container of padi (unhusked rice) filled to overflowing to symbolize a long life and plenty of good things in life; a sharp instrument, usually a knife, standing upright in the padi symbolizing protection against evil (a girl is thought to be in a state of spiritual danger from evil spirits at this time); and a lighted lamp to symbolize gaiety, brightness and cheerfulness in her personality. Finally the girl is given a container holding a whole coconut with some husk still covering the shell. It sits on some mango leaves. A bright red dot is painted on the centre of it to ward off the evil eye. She gives this to her uncle and his wife as a form of thanks. She is then given gifts of gold or money (in uneven amounts, e.g. $11, $21, etc.) by relatives and friends. After the ceremony the girl is taken to be bathed and her sari is given away so that she may never wear it again. The guests are invited to eat a vegetarian meal.

Usually only close friends and relatives are invited to witness this ceremony.

Indian boys do not normally have a tradition of circumcision, nor do they go through puberty rituals.

Etiquette for Puberty Celebrations
1   *Gifts:* If invited to a ceremony like this, bring the same type of gift that is mentioned above, i.e. gold or money.
2   *Dress:* Women should be dressed modestly. Men can be casually dressed in slacks and sports shirts.

COURTSHIP AND DATING

Young Indians, especially young Indian women, do not ordinarily date. They often mix in groups at school or with friends, but single dating is not encouraged. The women are securely protected by their families for their virtue is highly esteemed. Modern and Westernized Indians have more freedom in this matter. University students are often more liberal in their attitudes, but even they are careful to observe the traditions and values of their own society. While most Indian marriages are arranged by the parents with the young people's consent, there are usually no objections if a young

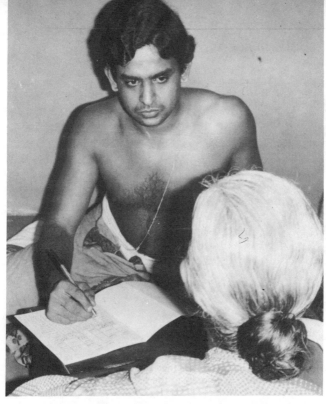

A temple priest helps to choose an auspicious date
for a wedding. *Photo: JoAnn Craig*

person chooses his or her own partner. However, it is
preferred that the marriage partner be of the same class,
caste and community as the young man or woman.

ENGAGEMENTS

For many Indians in Singapore and Malaysia, the
engagement, which takes place a few months before the
wedding, is almost like a small wedding. A close family friend
usually acts as a go-between. (It is considered delicate for a go-
between to handle negotiations between the two families.) A
priest chooses an auspicious date according to the horoscopes

The tree-planting ceremony. The aunts help prepare the tree that the couple will plant as a symbol of their new life together. Note the men and women sitting separately in the background. *Photo courtesy of Mr and Mrs G. Krishnan*

of the boy and girl. The engagement is usually held at the girl's home and the boy's party (his parents, relatives and friends) are officially welcomed by the girl's parents.

The girl, dressed almost like a bride, sits on a mat with her parents on either side. A tray of coconuts, flowers, oil lamps, etc. is placed before her. A priest may be present to bless the couple, and the go-between announces the engagement as the couple exchange rings. From then on, the couple may date. Propriety must still be observed however and the girl has to be home at a reasonable hour and should behave decorously.

Engagement Etiquette for Guests
1   Close relatives may bring gifts, but friends usually do not.
2   Women should be dressed modestly, their legs covered. Men dress casually.

WEDDINGS

Traditional Indians marry within their own class, caste and community. An Indian boy can marry his father's sister's daughter or his mother's brother's daughter (called cross-cousins by anthropologists). He cannot marry his father's brother's daughter or his mother's sister's daughter (called parallel cousins). Parallel cousins are considered almost as close as brothers and sisters. Southern Indians (patrilineal) often prefer the son to marry his mother's brother's daughter and Malayalees (matrilineal) often prefer the son to marry his father's sister's daughter. Uncle-niece marriages are also allowed in the Indian culture. (Note: Today, many modern Indians prefer their children to marry outside the family.)

Most marriages are negotiated by go-betweens on the instructions of the parents and with the consent of the children. The average marriage age for girls is 22-23 years; for boys it is around 25-28 years. Marriage in the Indian community is seen as sacred and eternal, lasting through life and even after! The symbols of a South Indian woman's marriage are a red dot on the forehead and the *thali,* a necklace that the husband ties around his wife's neck at the wedding. (North Indian symbols of marriage are bangles on the arm and a red streak on the woman's hair parting).

Some Indians have very simple ceremonies, some modern couples going to the extent of requesting the priest to shorten the ceremony to the barest minimum time possible, but traditional South Indians have elaborate affairs, sometimes lasting several hours. Sometime in the middle of the wedding, there is a tree-planting ceremony. The young couple plant a small tree in a little pot to symbolize their new life; if they have a garden, it is replanted there and it is a good sign if the plant flourishes! After the tree-planting ceremony, the couple change their clothes. The bride wears a completely new outfit given to her by the groom. It symbolizes that she is now his responsibility. Women who are noted for their happily

Tying the *thali*. The *thali* is as symbolic of the Indian wedding as the ring is of the Western marriage. At this sacred moment, the guests are careful not to sneeze as it would be a bad omen! *Photo courtesy of Mr and Mrs G. Krishnan*

married lives are the ones chosen to dress the bride, for the belief is that some of their happiness will rub off on her. The main part of the ceremony is the couple's walk round the holy fire, which represents a purifying element.

When the *thali* is tied, drums will be beaten wildly to drown any noises, sneezes, howling of dogs, etc., which are considered to be bad omens. Guests walk past the couple and throw yellow rice, a symbol of fertility, at them. (The rice is passed around so that each guest can throw a little.) As they pass, some may give presents of money or jewellery if they have not already done so.

After the wedding, the couple spends the first night in the

groom's home. An oil lamp will be lit to welcome them. The couple is advised to step over the threshold with the right foot to get off on the "right start". A warm, loving and sensual married life is highly valued in the Indian community and when newly-married couples visit friends or relatives they are given something sweet to ensure the sweetness of their life together.

Etiquette at Weddings

1 Guests should arrive on time and leave about half an hour after dinner is over.

2 A member of the family will accept gifts at the wedding or at the reception that may follow. Gifts can be given to the bride in person by visiting her home some time before the wedding.

3 Gifts for the home are appropriate, but something ornamental as well as functional is preferred. Money can be given in an envelope with a traditional wedding card. The amount is really up to the giver's discretion but odd numbers are more auspicious for Indians. A dollar is often added to an even amount to make it uneven: $21, $31, $51, etc.

4 Western women should dress smartly but modestly in ankle-length clothes: no plunging, backless or strapless gowns. Indian women usually come in beautiful glittering saris and heavy gold jewellery. Avoid white and black— the funeral colours; bright colours are correct for weddings. Men dress casually, usually in slacks and sports shirts.

5 Shoes should be removed at the temple door if the ceremony is held at a temple. Heads should be covered in the case of Sikh ceremonies, uncovered for the other Indian groups. (Note: *Men,* as well as women, *must* cover the head at a Sikh wedding!)

6 Guests should not sneeze while the *thali* is being tied. (It is a bad omen to sneeze at any important occasion or

business deal, etc. It is a sign that the venture will fail.)

7   Music will be played but there will be no dancing for the guests.

8   If the reception is held in a temple hall, vegetarian food may be served. Guests will normally eat with the fingers of the right hand. Western guests may be offered forks and spoons, but if they are not readily available, they should be prepared to eat with their right hand. If there are only a few chairs in the hall, the guests usually eat standing. If long tables are provided for the wedding lunch or dinner, do not leave the table until the persons on either side of you have left.

BIRTHS

For twenty-eight days after the birth of a baby, both mother and child are considered to be in a state of spiritual danger. The mother will have many restrictions placed on her: she will be put on a strict diet; she won't be allowed to leave her home, not even to visit the temple; her body will be wrapped every day, and, during her bath, hot water will be thrown on her stomach to shrink the womb.

The child is not called by name until the twenty-eighth day. At this time, the child is considered to be out of danger and there is usually a celebration to which friends and relatives are invited. The child will be placed on the father's lap, or on the lap of some relative, and his name will be whispered gently into his ears. From then on, he will be known and called by that name.

For several months after the birth of the baby, the mother will gently rub his head to mould it into a perfect shape: the forehead will be smoothed and flattened, the upper lip shaped and the bridge of the nose massaged to thin and refine it. The child's eyes will be rubbed with "Eye-tex" every day, in a circular motion around the rim of the upper and lower lids.

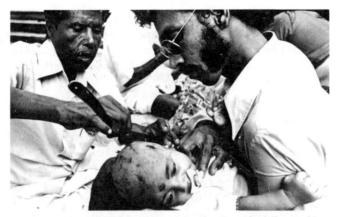

A mother's vow fulfilled. In thanksgiving for the safe delivery of her baby, this little one is having his head shaved at the temple. At all major Indian festivals, babies are brought to the temple to fulfil their mother's vow to the Divine Mother by having their birth-hair shaved. *Photo: Straits Times, Singapore*

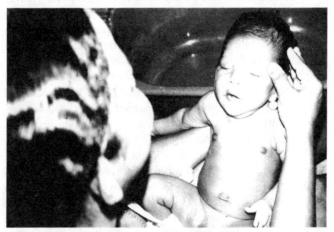

For the first six months of this baby's happy life, he will be given a special bath every morning. First he is gently rubbed with "gingelly oil". After resting for a few minutes, the mother cradles him on her legs while she lovingly caresses and massages his head, face, arms, legs and body. He is then washed in a little tub, breastfed, and put down for a long morning nap. *Photo: JoAnn Craig*

The skin at the side of the eye is gently stretched. This is believed to make the eyes large and round. The baby's body will also be massaged with "gingelly oil". An older woman will teach a young mother to do these things properly.

Etiquette for Births

1   It is not auspicious to visit a new mother on a Tuesday.
2   Gifts are usually not presented to the mother. Gold jewellery—a small chain, ring, bracelet or anklet—is often given to the baby.
3   A new mother will often give a sweet to visitors, especially if it is a first child, to express the sweetness in her life.

FUNERALS

Indians believe that when a person dies, the soul usually leaves the vicinity of the house only on the sixteenth day; some, who are very attached to their families, will linger on to the fortieth day. That is why an oil lamp is left burning in the home day and night (the light is the symbol of the soul) as a gesture of respect to the soul. Indians also believe in reincarnation. A man or woman will be reborn to make up for any harmful deed during his previous existence. He thus has an opportunity to purify and sanctify his spirit. His spiritual goal is to reach a state of perfection and enlightenment.

The funeral is usually held in the home of the deceased. Someone in the community who knows about funeral ceremonies will be called in to help with the formalities. The oldest son usually bathes the father and women bathe the body of a deceased woman. The body is dressed in new clothes and laid in a wooden coffin and silver coins are laid on the eyes to close them. Two oil lamps will be placed at either end of the coffin. Grandchildren and children walk around the coffin carrying lighted candles.

The body does not remain in the house for longer than

twelve hours. Most adults are cremated, children are not. If a man dies, a lady who has also lost her husband will step forward to remove the *thali* from around the widow's neck; it symbolizes the ending of the woman's married life. The red dot symbolizing her marriage is ceremoniously wiped off her forehead. The Northern Indian widow will strike her bangles against an object to break them. Although grief can be expressed, there is usually no loud wailing or keening.

Etiquette at Funerals

1   The caller pays his respects to the widow or widower first. He then stands by the body. It is appropriate to clasp the hands and to bow the head. A silent prayer can be said. He may then move away to make room for other visitors.

2   Only males may go to the crematorium. Transport may be provided. The female relatives of the deceased's family usually remain behind to clean the house, as is the custom after a deceased person has left the home.

3   Floral wreaths can be sent to the home. Usually, no money is given.

4   Sombre colours are appropriate: white, black, greyish or pale colours. Avoid bright, cheerful clothes.

5   A visitor can leave after paying respects; there is no special time to leave.

Funeral Taboos

Indians have certain taboos connected with funerals:

1   A visit to the family of the deceased should not be made on a Monday, Tuesday, or Thursday. The sorrow would come back to you!

2   After a funeral, the Indian does not enter the home before washing himself with some water left outside for this purpose. In fact, he will not drink, eat, talk or touch anyone until he has bathed.

3   Indians cannot attend a wedding and a funeral within the

same period of time. They have to choose one or the other.

4   A widow cannot visit the temple for a year after the death of her husband. A child may not go to the temple for a month after the death of a parent.

5   A widow cannot attend any social function for a year.

6   The family cannot consume meat for a certain period after the death of a family member.

6 Culture Shock — The Mysterious Malady

In a recent survey on culture shock conducted among expatriates in Singapore and Malaysia, a very startling thing came up. *Nearly one-half of the expatriates questioned had the wrong idea of it!*

Many of the expats had not even thought about it; many did not know the signs or symptoms; many felt that they had never experienced it; many did not know the stages of culture shock or the reactions of expats to it. Few knew how to recover from it. One lady summed up the general feeling about culture shock among expatriates with this statement: "I think that too much is made of culture shock!"

Since culture shock can almost be considered as an occupational disease of people who have been suddenly transplanted abroad, and because it is a malady which afflicts most expats to some degree, these responses were surprising indeed!

Because of the confusion that surrounds the mystery of culture shock, I would like to make some remarks about it.

What Do Many Expats Think Culture Shock Is?

Forty-five per cent of the expats surveyed *wrongly* thought that culture shock had to do with being "shocked", angered and disgusted by the differences they encountered in a foreign culture. This is not true. While these feelings may be felt by some expats, and while they do have some connection with culture shock (as some reactions to it) they are certainly not the phenomenon of culture shock itself. The confusion has most probably arisen because of the use of the term "shock".

What Does Culture Shock Mean?

The term "shock", when used in relation to culture shock, means: an impact; a sudden and disturbing physical or mental impression; a disturbance in the equilibrium of something. To clarify the confusion caused by the use of this misleading word "shock", I will refer to the malady of culture shock from this point on as *Culture Impact.*

Culture impact then has to do with a sudden and disturbing physical or mental impression that one encounters when coming into contact with a foreign culture. *Culture impact is, in fact, a state of stress and anxiety that results from the disturbing impressions we get and the loss of equilibrium we feel when we lose all our familiar signs and symbols of social intercourse, and when we encounter physical and environmental differences in an alien culture.* It can be compared to the feeling of being a fish out of water; or it can be likened to the phenomenon of "Stranger Anxiety"—the peculiar feeling we get when everyone in a society knows just what to do and how, why, where and when to do it, except the expat. And, of course, it is always the expat who must adjust and not the others.

Kalervo Oberg, an anthropologist attached to an ICA mission in Brazil, captured the big psychic trouble that losing our signs and symbols can cause when he wrote a memorandum that is now being used in many overseas training programs.

". . . these signs or cues include the thousand and one ways in which we orient ourselves to the situations of daily life: when to shake hands and what to say when we meet people, when and how to give tips, how to give orders to servants, how to make purchases, when to accept and when to refuse invitations, when to take statements seriously and when not. Now these cues which may be words, gestures, facial expressions, customs or norms are acquired by all of us in the course of growing up and are as much a part of our culture as the language we speak or the beliefs we accept. All of us depend for our peace of mind and our efficiency on hundreds of these cues, most of which we are not consciously aware of.

"Now when an individual enters a strange culture, all or most of these familiar cues are removed. No matter how broadminded or full of goodwill he may be, a series of props have been knocked from under him. This is followed by a feeling of frustration, stress and anxiety."[1]

Some Psychological Symptoms of the Culture Impact Syndrome

When the expat starts acting a bit peculiar, he is probably experiencing some of the symptoms of culture impact. Some of these symptoms have been reported by Kalervo Oberg: "Excessive concern over cleanliness and the feeling that what is new and strange is *dirty*. This could be in relation to drinking water, food, dishes, and bedding; fear of physical contact with locals or servants; a feeling of helplessness and a desire for dependence on long-term residents of one's own nationality; irritation over delays and other minor frustrations, out of proportion to their causes; delay and outright refusal to learn the customs and habits of the host country; excessive fear of being cheated, robbed or injured; great concern over minor pains and eruptions of the skin; and finally, that terrible longing to be back home, to be in familiar surroundings, to visit one's relatives, and in general, to talk to people *who really make sense*."[2]

Other anthropologists have included a few more symptoms to this list: excessive washing of hands, the absent-minded faraway stare, excessive fatigue, and excessive drinking.

Do Most Expatriates in Singapore and Malaysia Fall Victim to Culture Impact?

Unfortunately, anthropological studies and recent surveys carried out show that they do! However, individuals differ greatly in the degree to which culture impact affects them. Although it is not common, there are some individuals who cannot live in foreign countries.

The average expat finds it easier to cope with the physical differences in a new culture—he can deal with them as he learns to build up a tolerance for differences in the environment. What he can *see,* he can handle.

The cultural differences are another story. They often hit the expat below the level of his consciousness. He is often not aware of what the cultural differences are, hence the feeling of many expatriates surveyed here who were not even aware of being victims of culture impact. What he is *not aware of,* he cannot handle.

In a survey carried out by the writer, 98 per cent of the expats in Singapore were found to be victims of culture impact. They experienced it in mild, moderate and severe degrees, and they experienced it in both the cultural and the physical areas.

The table opposite shows the percentage of *severe* culture impact that different types of expats experienced. (Note: This table does not show the degree of mild and moderate culture impact.)

As we can see, there are several interesting and provocative thoughts in the table!

1 First-timers experience a lot more culture impact than the Old-timers. It is what one would expect.

2 The most striking comparison in the whole table is the one between the Quei-lo's and the Westerners. It appears that

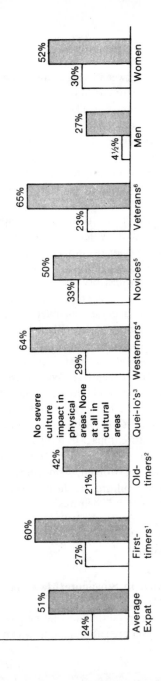

SOME DIFFERENT TYPES OF EXPATS AND
HOW CULTURE IMPACT IS MEDIATED BY THEIR EXPERIENCES

☐ severe culture impact in
physical and environmental areas

▨ severe culture impact
in cultural areas

Average Expat 51% 24%

First-timers[1] 60% 27%

Old-timers[2] 42% 21% (No severe culture impact in physical areas. None at all in cultural areas)

Quei-lo's[3] 64% 29%

Westerners[4] 64% 29%

Novices[5] 50% 33%

Veterans[6] 65% 23%

Men 27% 4½%

Women 52% 30%

1   First-timers: Expats who have never lived in a foreign country before coming here. (35 per cent)

2   Old-timers: Expats who have lived in a foreign country (Eastern and/or Western) before coming here. (65 per cent)

3   Quei-lo's: Expats who have lived in a foreign *Asian* country before coming here. (20 per cent)

4   Westerners: Expats who have lived in a foreign *Western* country before coming here. (45 per cent)

5   Novices: Expats who have lived in Singapore or Malaysia for *less* than six months. (35 per cent)

6   Veterans: Expats who have lived in Singapore or Malaysia for *more* than six months.

there is a connection between living in an *Asian* country
before coming to Singapore or Malaysia and a successful
experience in these countries! The Quei-lo does suffer
from culture impact, but only in a mild or moderate
degree. *He suffers no severe culture impact at all.*

The Westerner, on the other hand, falls victim to a very
high degree of severe culture impact. An expatriate's *first*
experience in an Asian culture is therefore likely to be
devastating.

3   Novices suffer from more physical culture impact than
any other type of expat. Veterans suffer from more
cultural culture impact than any other type of expat. This
strange phenomenon can be explained. Oddly enough,
Veterans are hit the hardest because they have lived in
Singapore or Malaysia long enough to have become
aware of many subliminal cultural problems and differences. They have usually become so confused by them that
they have retreated into "culture bubbles" with their own
countrymen, and rejected the host society. They have
actually seen below the deceptively Westernized surface
of the modern skyscrapers and noticed a decidedly Asian
psyche here—but are at a loss as to what to do about it.

4   Another amazing fact is the visible proof that women
suffer much more culture impact in both areas than men
do. There will be more on this later, but for now it is
enough to say that the women, who come into daily
contact with the Asian culture, are the ones who have the
least help in coping with it. Their husbands are insulated
more or less by their exciting job experiences and their
day-to-day dealings with Westernized business practices
and helpful compatriots.

The Profile of the Expat in Singapore/Malaysia and their Symptoms of Culture Impact

Since so many of the cultural differences in the environment
of Singapore and Malaysia are subliminal, how can he tell if

he falls victim to culture impact? Below is a typical picture (taken from the survey) of the average and unsuspecting expat.

Mr and Mrs Average Expat are between the ages of 35 and 45. They both have high educational qualifications. The survey shows that 70 per cent of the women have attended at least one to three years of university and some have even gone on to higher qualifications. Mr Expat is more highly qualified educationally than his wife: the survey shows that 70 per cent of the men have finished university, and 59 per cent have gone on to further qualifications.

Mr Expat is more likely to be an executive businessman (42 per cent) or a skilled engineer or oil construction technician (29 per cent). The other 29 per cent are a combination of professionals, missionaries and military or embassy personnel. Mrs Expat, even though she may possess a university degree (mostly in teaching and nursing), does not work in Singapore and Malaysia because of the ruling of the Ministry of Labour in these countries.

Mrs Expat finds that some of the hardest things to get used to in Singapore and Malaysia are some of the silliest little things: like where to find a good hairdresser; what kind of tinned tomatoes can replace her old standby; how to work the new stove that has Centigrade gas-marks on it instead of Fahrenheit markings; how to get used to driving on the left side of the road, manoeuvre roundabouts, and cope with Asian driving etiquette (or lack of it). She also has problems in dealing with her servant. (How to lie on the sofa and read while someone else is cleaning up her house? Better to go shopping while the *amah* is here!) She finds it impossible to understand why the television repairman has not come when he "promised" he would come. She is confused about setting up her new home: "What do you mean, the water heaters don't come with the apartment . . . we're paying $2500 a month for it!" The climate "throws" her for the first few months: she can't understand why she is always so tired. She misses the seasonal changes but loves to see the sun shining every day. She is upset by cockroaches that are as big as field mice, and she faints when the *cicaks* leap out of her cooking pot as she reaches for it! She keeps a never-ending surveillance against the ants that really don't stop coming. She gets really cross when she sees mildew covering her new leather bag and shoes. She'll never get used to seeing hawkers hanging up cooked chickens and ducks — "Right in the open air!" Squat toilets are a mystery to her; chances are she has never seen one before she came to Singapore or Malaysia! Bathing from a well and sitting side-saddle takes practice in rural Malaysia! However, she soon learns to take all these things in her stride as she builds up her tolerance for physical differences.

Mr Expat doesn't worry so much about all these things; after all, he is very busy working at the office all day, or else travelling "out of town". What he finds hardest to get used to are the differences in humour, frankness, reserve; the differences in work habits, methods, attitudes, company structure, chain of command, authority, local business practices; and the locals' tendency to say "yes" when they mean "I hear what you say, but I don't necessarily agree".

They both find it difficult to bargain in shops; to answer questions like: "How much did you pay?"; and to contain their expressions of anger, over-friendliness, exuberance and tone of voice. They also find it difficult to stop "touching" people.

Culture impact hits Mr and Mrs Expat hardest in the cultural areas when they suddenly realize that something has gone wrong in their conversation with their local friend. "What was that funny expression for?" "Did that sudden twist of the neck on the old gentleman mean something?" "Not five minutes ago we were all laughing and happy, and now I'm sure I can feel a change in the vibrations here!" Mr and Mrs Expat have just realized that their assumptions have not been met by their local friend! In Singapore and Malaysia this realization often comes as a "hunch" or an "intuition". Few of the locals would make a guest in their country feel embarrassed by calling social blunders and cultural-foot-in-mouth errors to their attention. The expat might notice a peculiar expression on the local's face, or he might see his local friend take a step backwards when he reaches to touch him. The expat may not know *why* something has gone wrong; or *how* he has caused something to go wrong; or even *what* has gone wrong. All he knows is that something definitely is taking place that he did not expect to take place! For example: Wanting to signal friendship and openness, Mr Expat is hugging or kissing his Asian hostess when he should not even be touching her; Mrs Expat is pinching the fat cheeks of the hostess's pretty baby while praising its health and good looks, when all Asian mothers know that this action is liable to be dangerous (the spirits may become jealous and take away the baby's charms through the "evil eye").

Wanting to impress the local ladies of her husband's staff at his Malay secretary's wedding, Mrs Expat is wearing her most lovely backless, sleeveless and plunging evening dress—she notices too late that all the Malay ladies are wearing very modest clothing that cover everything but their head, hands and feet. The intrepid expat is standing too close; he is laughing at the wrong things; he is sneezing at the wrong times; he is calling his colleague by his first name; he is conveying anger by speaking loudly, when he thinks that he is only being "firm". Mr Expat is walking into his Indian partner's home with his shoes on without noticing that everyone else in the house has removed his shoes. Junior Expat is handing a sandwich to his Malay friend with the left hand, not noticing the "surprised" look on his face! (Junior doesn't realize that Malays and Indians never use the left hand for social purposes.) Mr Expat is inadvertently making an extremely obscene gesture in front of his host's wife and children by soundly slapping his fist against his left palm, not knowing that there is a taboo against making that kind of gesture.

Wanting to express joy to her Chinese friend who has just given birth to a new baby, Mrs Expat brings her a lovely floral arrangement, complete with a stork nestled in it (she has spent a considerable amount of time trying to find a stork in the shops). She doesn't know why her friend reacts with "unease" (the flowers and stork symbolize sickness and death).

It is precisely at times like these that the expat realizes that "culture" is "real" and that it is "learned". It is also at times like these that the expat comes to understand that people are not necessarily bound by universal common denominators of "human nature" into patterns of mutual understanding. The expat finally comes to understand what Confucius meant when he said: "All people are the same, *it's only their habits* that are so different!"

How Do Expats React to Culture Impact?

Expats ease their adjustment to a foreign culture by reacting in certain ways. The reactions are so common that anthropologists can predict pretty accurately how most expats will respond to culture impact!

During the first few weeks, most individuals are fascinated by the new. They stay in hotels and associate with people who are polite and gracious to them. This honeymoon stage may last from a few days or weeks to six months.[3]

What happens after this stage can be seen in the following models. (They are idealistic ones, and not intended to be realistic. The boundaries overlap, and no one expat can be said to fit the pattern exactly.) The type of response an expat makes during the early stages often determines the type of expat he will turn out to be.

The Encapsulator

The most common garden-variety type of expat is the Encapsulator. He makes his adjustment mostly to the expatriate culture. He experiences minimum contact with the local culture and the local people. He learns very little about the customs and traditions of the host society, and has very little to do with the people of the foreign society, except on a superficial level. He lives in Singapore or Malaysia, but never experiences the culture.

He tends to "clump together" with other expats of his own kind into ready-made "culture bubbles" for security and emotional support. He usually lives in an expat area, joins the expat clubs, shops at the stores that cater to the expat's tastes, and sends his children to the expat schools. The expatriate culture is made up of a web of social relationships in which expats meet and mix with each other through work, socials, leisure, sports, clubs and religious functions.

The Encapsulator becomes a part of a miniature "Little America", "Little England", "Little Holland", etc. He does not have to face the problems of learning a new culture, but seeks instead to learn how to live the *expatriate way of life*. While this type of adjustment may be beneficial to the expat, as it can help him to "settle in" with the least amount of difficulty, and to face the least amount of cultural disorientation, it can be harmful in the extreme because it can cause him to become insular. The ready-made culture bubble can prevent him from learning about the local culture, and it can prevent him from making personal and close contacts with local people—it can prevent him from making a successful cultural adaptation.

The Encapsulator does not make the most effective use of his exposure to a new culture. He often does not learn how to live and work successfully among the local people or how to have successful business relationships with them. He also does not adjust well to living in a foreign culture. In the survey, 67 per cent of the expats have been identified as Encapsulators.

The Reactions of the Encapsulator to the Foreign Environment

(a) *Flight*

Many expats who become Encapsulators have succumbed to the *flight* syndrome in reacting to culture impact. They run away from what is strange and unfamiliar to them; or they avoid the host culture. Flight comes in three stages: rejection, regression and retreatism.

(i) REJECTION. They reject the environment which causes the discomfort: "The ways of the host country are bad because they make us feel bad." Whenever you find expats sitting around grousing about the foreign culture, you can be sure they are suffering the "rejection" reaction to culture impact! This rejection and hostility grow out of the genuine difficulty which the expat experiences in the process of adjustment. There are all kinds of troubles to cope with: mail trouble, school, housing, transportation, shopping, communication troubles, etc. The host people try to help, but they just don't understand the expat's great concern over these troubles. Therefore, the expat feels they must be unsympathetic to him and his worries.

(ii) REGRESSION. They have a relapse back to the time when they were happy and secure in their own country. They start to glorify irrationally everything about their home country. They remember only "the good old days back when . . ." They start to compare unfavourably all the aspects in the alien society to the wonderful aspects of their own country. They forget all the problems they had experienced then and only remember the good things. It usually takes a trip back on home-leave to bring them back to their senses.[4] This is a critical period of adjustment. It is crucial during this stage that the expat develops an understanding and acceptance of the host culture, and makes close contact with local people. If he makes a successful adjustment during this period he can go on to become a happy and contented Cosmopolitan. If he fails to make the adjustment, he will go on to the "Retreatism" stage where he may remain for the duration of his overseas assignment.

(iii) RETREATISM. The third and final stage is complete when they isolate themselves from the alien culture that they do not understand—the culture that causes them frustration,

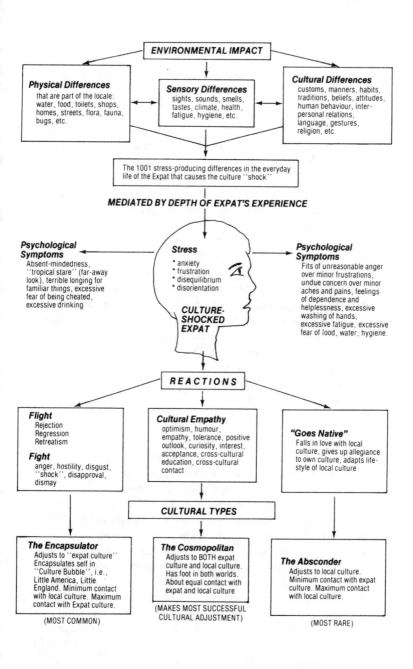

ENVIRONMENTAL IMPACT

Physical Differences
that are part of the locale: water, food, toilets, shops, homes, streets, flora, fauna, bugs, etc.

Sensory Differences
sights, sounds, smells, tastes, climate, health, fatigue, hygiene, etc.

Cultural Differences
customs, manners, habits, traditions, beliefs, attitudes, human behaviour, interpersonal relations, language, gestures, religion, etc.

The 1001 stress-producing differences in the everyday life of the Expat that causes the culture "shock"

MEDIATED BY DEPTH OF EXPAT'S EXPERIENCE

Psychological Symptoms
Absent-mindedness, "tropical stare" (far-away look), terrible longing for familiar things, excessive fear of being cheated, excessive drinking

Stress
* anxiety
* frustration
* disequilibrium
* disorientation

CULTURE-SHOCKED EXPAT

Psychological Symptoms
Fits of unreasonable anger over minor frustrations, undue concern over minor aches and pains, feelings of dependence and helplessness, excessive washing of hands, excessive fatigue, excessive fear of food, water, hygiene.

REACTIONS

Flight
Rejection
Regression
Retreatism

Fight
anger, hostility, disgust, "shock", disapproval, dismay

Cultural Empathy
optimism, humour, empathy, tolerance, positive outlook, curiosity, interest, acceptance, cross-cultural education, cross-cultural contact

"Goes Native"
Falls in love with local culture, gives up allegiance to own culture, adapts lifestyle of local culture

CULTURAL TYPES

The Encapsulator
Adjusts to "expat culture". Encapsulates self in "Culture Bubble", i.e., Little America, Little England. Minimum contact with local culture. Maximum contact with Expat culture.

(MOST COMMON)

The Cosmopolitan
Adjusts to BOTH expat culture and local culture. Has foot in both worlds. About equal contact with expat and local culture

(MAKES MOST SUCCESSFUL CULTURAL ADJUSTMENT)

The Absconder
Adjusts to local culture. Minimum contact with expat culture. Maximum contact with local culture.

(MOST RARE)

anxiety, disorientation and pain. They join the expat culture of their countrymen and take refuge in its cocktail circuit.

(b) *Fight*

Some expats also experience the *fight* syndrome in reacting to culture impact. They respond to the differences in the new culture with anger, hostility, dismay, disgust, disapproval and frustration. People in a foreign culture have habits of their own that are different from the expat's habits. They often break his habits, and habit-breaking is unpleasant. When expats confront "strange" habits, they often retreat from them and seek out people of their own kind who have similar habits.[5]

Instead of trying to account for conditions as they are through an honest analysis of the actual conditions and the historical circumstances which have created them, the expat talks as if the difficulties were more or less created by the people of the host society for the expat's special discomfort. The use of stereotypes, such as "the dollar-grasping Chinese", may salve the ego of an expat with a severe case of culture impact, but it does not lead to an understanding of the host country and its people.[6]

The Cosmopolitan

This type of expat is a pretty rare species (only 27 per cent of the expats surveyed were identified as Cosmopolitans), and not too often seen in foreign countries. Though he is not so common, he is the one who makes the most successful adjustment to living and working in a foreign culture. He makes his adjustment to the local culture as well as to the expat culture. He has a foot in both worlds, so to speak! The Cosmopolitan meets and mixes equally with people from both cultures. He learns about the differences that befuddle him in the foreign culture so that he can understand them and feel comfortable in the society. He develops the skill to understand the inner logic and coherence of other ways of life and the restraint not to judge them as bad because they are different from his own ways.[7]

The Cosmopolitan accepts the fact that cultures are relative and he learns to appreciate the host culture for what it is: he doesn't try to fight it or to change it. He does not go "native", or give up his own system of values or beliefs. On the contrary, he retains his own loyalties to his values and his allegiance to his country. He does not feel that loyalty to his own country excludes a loyalty to his host country. He expands and stretches his attitudes and etiquette to include those of his host's in the name of friendship and goodwill. He may never learn to love fish-heads, *belacan* or durian, but he is considerate and respectful towards the people of his host country and he appreciates their culture.

The Cosmopolitan can usually be identified by his optimism, enthusiasm, humour, high self-concept, and his positive respect for individuals, whoever they are. Gordon Allport calls this type of personality the "Tolerant Personality".[8]

This type of expat reacts to cultural dislocation with empathy, curiosity, interest and acceptance. He takes positive steps to learn about the culture and to meet the people. He actively seeks information, asks questions, and reads books about the culture. He makes friends with local people on an equal-status basis. He can operate within the new culture without feeling stress and anxiety, although there will still be moments of strain. Only with a complete grasp of all the cues of social intercourse will all strain disappear.[9]

He experiences his stay in the foreign culture with joy, and when he leaves the country, a part of the people and the culture goes with him . . . and a part of him stays with them.

The Cosmopolitan often has less difficulty in adjusting to the other problems that accompany a transplanting, i.e., business, personal, emotional and familial problems.

The Absconder

This type of expat is the most rare of all, but he does in fact exist. Some examples of this type were the sailors of Captain Bligh who mutinied in order to stay with their Tahitian women. Anthropologists talk about this type when they refer to those anthropologists who "go native, put on loin-cloths, and dance around tom-toms"! Some young people in the Peace Corps also became absconders when they went to live with local people in rural areas, learned their language, and adapted their life-style. Some of them forgot how to speak their own native tongue and found it difficult to readjust to living in their own country.

The Absconder does in fact "turn native". He restricts his relationships to those of the local people in the community. He has minimum contact with people of his own culture. He makes his maximum adjustment to the local culture.

He may marry into the local community; take up citizenship in the local country; put down roots in the new culture. He considers the local community to be "home" and he gives up allegiance to his own country.[10] This type of expat often ceases to be an expat according to the definition of an expat in the context of this book. (Expatriate: a foreign national living and working in a third-world foreign country for more than six months who considers his country of residence as alien, and his country of origin as home.)[11] He becomes an expatriate in the sense of the Webster's definition: "one who renounces allegiance to one's native country" (a cultural turncoat).

The Absconder reacts to cultural dislocation with a sense of euphoria. He may "fall in love" with the local culture and choose to remain there rather than return to his own country.

The survey did not turn up any Absconders, but there was a figure of 6 per cent for missionaries who live on the local level, mix mostly with local people, and identify themselves as "becoming more a part of the local culture than the expat one". However, the missionaries cannot be considered to be

Absconders because they have not given up their allegiance to their native country.

What Can You Do to Get Over Culture Impact as Quickly as Possible?

I *A part of the answer is to learn as much as you can about the customs, the habits, the culture, the patterns of everyday behaviour, the manners, the attitudes and the religion of the people of Singapore and Malaysia.* Once you realize that the trouble of culture impact is due to your *own* lack of communicating with the cues, signs and symbols of your *own* culture, rather than the hostility of an alien environment, you will realize that you yourself can gain this understanding and the means to social intercourse through study and learning. [12]

Unfortunately, most of your study will have to be done on an individual level. Research has shown that there is very little information available, and very little help given by multinational corporations, embassies, or expatriate communities. (Only 16 per cent of the corporations here offered cultural orientation to their expats.)

Some Self-help Methods of Learning the Culture:
1 Take classes in the culture and languages of the host country whenever possible. The universities and the expat clubs often offer classes to which the public are invited.
2 Talk to the locals, ask them to teach you the do's and don'ts, the whys and the hows!
3 Read books to help you understand the Malaysian and Singaporean psyche. Some titles are suggested here:
    (a) Etiquette and Customs:
       (i) *Culture Shock! Singapore and Malaysia,* J. Craig

    (b) Religion:
- (i) *The Great Religions by which Men Live*, Ross and Hills
- (ii) *What the Great Religions Believe*, Joseph Gaer

    (c) Festivals
- (i) *A Cycle of Chinese Festivities*, C.K. Wong
- (ii) *Festivals of Malaya*, Joy Manson (edit.)
- (iii) Copies of *Asia* and *Orientation* magazines, and the back issues of *The Straits Times Annual*

    (d) History and Non-Fiction (Singapore)
- (i) *Son of Singapore*, Tan Kok Seng
- (ii) *Sinister Twilight*, Noel Barber
- (iii) *King Rat*, James Clavell
- (iv) *When Singapore Was Syonan-to*, N.I. Low
- (v) *Syonan—My Story*, M. Shinozaki

    (e) History and Non-Fiction (Malaysia)
- (i) *Man of Malaysia*, Tan Kok Seng
- (ii) *Modern Malaysian Chinese Stories*, Ly Jingke
- (iii) *No Harvest but a Thorn*, Shannon Ahmad
- (iv) *War of the Running Dogs*, Noel Barber
- (v) *The Jungle is Neutral*, F. Spencer Chapman
- (vi) *A Town Like Alice*, Nevil Shute

    (f) Expatriate Living Conditions in Singapore
- (i) *Living in Singapore*, American Association of Singapore

    (g) Any of the good tourists books.

II   *The rest of the answer lies in getting to know the people of Singapore and Malaysia. Find out what they do, why and how they do things, and what their interests are. Form close friendships with them on an equal-status basis. Have shared and common goals.*[13]

    1   If you cannot work or study with them, or live in the

same areas with them, then let your hobbies help you. Go where they go!

(a) Join the Kennel Club. Have your child take the family dog to obedience or handling classes.
(b) Join a local photo club.
(c) Take a local language course. (Most people say that Malay is the easiest to learn!)
(d) Join the Stage Club or the Experimental Theatre.
(e) Take an extra-mural class at the university.
(f) Learn how to cook Malay, Chinese or Indian food.
(g) Learn how to make batik, weave or paint.
(h) Send your child to Kung Fu classes.
(i) The local community centres offer a variety of classes on all kinds of hobbies.
(j) The local YMCA offers many classes and activities to expats as well as locals.

2 SPORTS
Golfing, sailing, tennis, cricket, squash, water-skiing, scuba-diving, nature walks, etc. are abundant in Singapore and Malaysia. Expand these interests to include local friends. What better way to meet locals than to work with them in the pursuit of common goals!

3 VOLUNTEER WORK
(a) The local school for the blind always needs people to help with "Talking Books".
(b) The Samaritans will train volunteers.
(c) The expat clubs usually have a roster of volunteer work that expats can make use of to find suitable volunteer work in the community.

4 Do try to work or attend classes. Women and teenagers, check with the Ministry of Labour to see if you have a special talent that can be used.

Finally, a word to fellow expats. Do what you can to help other expats recover from culture impact. It is well to recognize that persons suffering from culture impact feel weak in the face of conditions which appear insurmountable, it is natural for them to try to lean heavily on their compatriots. This may be irritating to the long-term resident, but he should be patient, sympathetic, and understanding. Although talking does not remove pain, a great deal is gained by having the source of pain explained.[14]

What About the Physical Differences Here?
Most expats learn how to cope with them quickly, but here are a few suggestions for newcomers to Singapore and Malaysia.

I   *Adjusting to the Physical Differences*
Malaysia and Singapore are only a short distance from the equator and the climate is hot and steamy. People often feel a sense of heaviness when they first come here. They tend to tire easily and often have a hard time staying awake during the day.

1   Rest and take things easy in the first few weeks after your arrival. Let your body acclimatize itself to the tropical conditions.

2   Pamper yourself in the beginning, but don't make a habit of it. Just realize that you won't have all the energy that you would normally have in your old environment. It will take a little time to adjust to the physical changes.

3   Relax! Slow down! Enjoy a lazier pace of life! Keep a cool head!

4   Some of the doctors at a missionary hospital in Singapore recommend an iron and yeast tablet as a daily supplement.

5   Try not to depend on air conditioners too much. It is difficult to acclimatize the body to the tropical climate here if one is constantly living in an artificially controlled environment. Fans are helpful.

THE MYSTERIOUS MALADY 187

6 Make allowances for the climate by preparing meals early in the day when it is cooler and you are feeling fresher. Use one of the "slow-cooking" pots, or refrigerate or freeze the meal and reheat it in the evening.

7 Don't be alarmed by the number of *cicaks* (little lizards) that you see in your home. They are believed to bring good luck. Besides, they eat up mosquitoes and other insects too! Some locals leave out little offerings of food to entice them to stay.

II *Adjusting to the Environmental Differences*

Coping with any change in environment is always difficult. It is best to try to get your bearings in the new city as quickly as possible.

1 Learn the areas of the city you live in. Become familiar with the streets and shopping districts. Study a map.

2 Take small bus trips to become familiar with the city. Just get on a bus and ride it to the end of the line.

3 Learn where to find doctors, beauty parlors, shopping centres and markets as quickly as you can. It will help ease your disorientation.

4 Learn how to convert the local currency.

5 Do comparison shopping in supermarkets before buying. Just familiarize yourself with prices, merchandise and local stock.

6 If you drive, be prepared for an entirely different set of driving habits and customs. If you have been used to driving on the right-hand side of the road, prepare yourself mentally for the change to driving on the left side. Every time you start the car, say to yourself: "Keep left, keep left".

7 It is a good idea to ask a local friend or an Old-timer expat to accompany you the first few times you drive here. They can explain details like bus lanes, roundabouts, zebra crossings, pedestrian rules, and so on.

8 Get a good street guide and start off by taking small trips

first. Don't be disconcerted by what appears to you to be reckless driving. Asians are used to people doing suicidal things while driving and they ordinarily make allowances for any mistakes that you might make.

Notes

1 Oberg, Kalervo, *Culture Shock and the Problem of Adjustment to New Cultural Environments,* International Publications, Foreign Service Institute, Department of State, Washington, D.C., December 1958.
2 Oberg, op. cit.
3 Oberg, op. cit.
4 Oberg, op. cit.
5 Allport, Gordon, *The Nature of Prejudice,* N.Y., Doubleday, 1958, p. 45.
6 Oberg, op. cit.
7 Cleveland, Mangone and Adams, *The Overseas American,* N.Y., McGraw-Hill, 1960, p. 136.
8 Allport, op. cit., pp. 398-412.
9 Oberg, op. cit.
10 Mayer, Philip, and Dova, *Townsmen or Tribesmen,* Capetown, Oxford University Press, 1974, pp. 6-9.
11 Clements, K.P., "The Expatriate as a Stranger", *The Voice,* University of Hong Kong Students Union, March 1973.
12 Oberg, op. cit.
13 Allport, op. cit., p. 454.
14 Oberg, op. cit.

7 Survival in Singapore/Malaysia — A Guide for Expats!

When an individual decides to live the expatriate style of life he faces the prospect of clashing with a double-edged sword. He is not only exposed to the "shock" (impact) of the foreign culture he will be living in, but he is also exposed to the "shock" (impact) of living the "Expatriate Life-style".

Expatriates do not live the normal, everyday style of life that is to be found in most surburbias of the world. They move from one place to another; they have no real place to call home; they are forever saying "hello" and "goodbye" to loved ones; they have to adjust to leaving old friends behind and they have to cope with making new friends. For them, nothing is permanent; they are like the wind, blowing through people's lives, with never a place to settle. They take their children with them, until they reach an age where they must return home, and then they go on without them! These modern-day nomads help to bridge the barriers between cultures in the world; they bring science and technology to underdeveloped countries; they hold the key to international peace and understanding in their briefcase or toolbox; they create business for their compatriots at home, and thereby create jobs for them. They also teach, train, organize, and guide local staff and workers to achieve economic independence. In the end, they leave a highly industrialized and modernized core of local technicians and industrialists in their wake—then they move on!

Expats receive pleasure from this style of life, of course, or else they would never do it. However, expats also receive pain from this vagabond existence.

WHAT ARE SOME OF THE PROBLEMS THAT THE EXPAT ENCOUNTERS IN LIVING OVERSEAS?

I THE FIRST PROBLEMS ARE EMOTIONAL

Depression, anxiety, disorientation, distraction, irritability, homesickness and loneliness are normal for the expatriate; they are to be expected when one is uprooted and transplanted into a strange and alien society. A survey of expatriates in Singapore showed that 56 per cent of them said they felt depression; 81 per cent said that loneliness was one of their biggest problems (leaving behind loved family, friends and adult children); 58 per cent said that they felt anxiety and disorientation; 76 per cent admitted frustration, stress, and strain on a daily basis. Note: Because of these stresses, and because of the difficulty of adjusting to the role of the "stranger" in a new society, excessive drinking can be a problem for men, women and teenagers. Expats often consume large amounts of alcohol as part of their leisure-time activities. Hard work, long hours away from home, the disappointments of cross-cultural operations, and the requirements for mutual entertaining make alcohol an occupational hazard for the expat.

Marital problems also have a tendency to multiply because of the stress of an unfamiliar and non-supportive culture. The maladjusted family in their own homeland has many more escape routes in which to accommodate their needs. Antagonistic elements, vaguely recognized at home, can become accentuated abroad.

We can see that most expats feel a bit strange for the first few months or so after a move into a new cultural milieu. Even the most seasoned of expats (the Old-timers) admit to experiencing many of these feelings. When one knows what to expect, one can deal much better with the emotional problems that are common to expatriates. *Awareness* often helps expatriates to recover from the stress of culture impact, as well as to overcome many of the emotional problems that accompany his style of life.

There is little advice that can mitigate all the emotional problems encountered by the expat, except awareness. The expat should be aware that these problems are normal, that nearly everyone goes through them; that they are temporary and transitory; that they pass as soon as the expat acclimatizes himself to the new culture and surroundings with the exception of loneliness which may continue to grow.

The expat can help himself to reduce these feelings and to shorten their duration by taking active steps to overcome them in several ways:

1 *By having a healthy and stable family relationship.*
2 *By developing a "Family Plan",* i.e., by working together as a family on a self-education programme. By helping each other to understand the culture and the conditions of life in the new culture, and by offering each other mutual support. (See "Family Plan", page 214.)
3 *By cultivating the traits of cultural empathy* (the ability to understand and appreciate the ways of the host country, and not judge them as bad because they are different from your own ways): tolerance, understanding, acceptance, humour and cultural relativity. (Of the expats surveyed who reported a successful and happy adjustment to their host country, 73 per cent were seen to have most or all of these personality traits.

4 *By learning the customs and by making close friends with locals.* (Through current research and scientific studies — this advice is the best that an expat can receive to reduce the stress and strain of culture impact, thus reducing concommitant emotional problems.)

Here is some advice, taken from a survey conducted by this author, that some First-timer and Old-timer expats would like to give to Newcomers:

1 "Accept the fact that you will not be able to change your new environment, or make it over into one that is closer to your own ideal."

2 "The biggest task of the new expat is to learn to feel at ease in the new culture—realize that this may take three or four months."

3 "Just remember that Singapore is not 'like home'—but it's most like home than anywhere overseas that we have been before."

4 "Come in with an open mind, and do not get too frazzled by all the differences in etiquette and customs."

5 "Realize that this is not your own home . . . accept it . . . adapt!"

6 "Get acquainted with local people as soon as possible."

7 "Learn Oriental Patience."

8 "Try to relate . . . Keep your eyes open and your mouth shut!"

9 "Join a church; adopt a positive attitude; realize that we are guests in this country. Read books, learn the customs."

10 "Be interested and see and do everything offered. Also make as many friends as possible."

11 "Be prepared for a period of adjustment and keep busy."

12 "Try to understand the Malaysian ways and find the good points. Soon you will see how wonderful they are!"

13 "Stay loose; keep cool; be open-minded."

14 "Don't try to do it all alone, seek God's help."

15 "Get your bearings first before rushing into life."

16 "Take it gently!"
17 "Don't keep comparing Singapore with your home country!"
18 "Learn about the country and the customs of Malaysia before moving there!"
19 "Be yourself. Take care of your family."
20 One Old-timer expat, Bob Wakefield, quotes a passage by Rudyard Kipling as his best advice for the Newcomer:

> It is not good for the Westerner's* health
> To hustle the Asian brown
> For the Westerner riles . . . and the Asian smiles
> And he weareth the Westerner down
> And the end of the fight is a tombstone white
> With the name of the late deceased
> And the epitaph drear: "A fool lies here
> Who tried to hustle the East."

For those of you who suffer from severe or prolonged depression, or if things seem very difficult to cope with, there is help in Singapore when you need a friend:

1 *SACAC* (Phone 468-1944): The Singapore American Community Action Council has trained personnel and counselling services available. Any request for assistance will be responded to. They deal mostly with teenagers, parents and individuals.

2 *The Counselling and Care Centre* (Phone 337-7748): this is a member of the Singapore Council of Social Services. This centre provides services to people of any race, nationality or creed. It provides services for the individual, the group, and also marital counselling.

3 *Samaritans of Singapore* (Phone 221-4444 — Emergency number): Trained volunteers answer a 24-hour answering service. They can put you on to where help is available for problems of alcoholism, despair, suicide.

---

* Bob has taken the liberty of changing Kipling's "Christian" to "Westerner".

In Kuala Lumpur, there is an extension of the services provided in Singapore at the:

Churches Counselling Centre (2 Jalan Wesley, K.L.): This centre combines two services: Care and Counselling and the Samaritans. They offer help to people of any race, nationality or creed.

II THE OTHER PROBLEMS HAVE TO DO WITH THE EXPAT LIFE-STYLE

Problems affect each member of the family. We'll look at some of the problems peculiar to each member.

A Men
1 Their Business Problems
Husbands have reported few problems in living overseas. It is often easier for the husband to adapt to life in a foreign culture than it is for the wife and children. The husband is caught up in the challenge of his new position. He meets daily with people who share the same business interests. He usually has a built-in "family" of professional and business associates. Working in a foreign culture often enhances his knowledge, experience and skill. He often makes more money than he would at home, and he experiences the pleasure of increased autonomy in his job and satisfaction and prestige as well. One expat says: "The job satisfaction is very good here. However, there is the likelihood of alienation from job opportunities at home."

(a) *Cultural Differences:* With all these bonuses and be-nefits, he may still fall victim to the differences in cultural habits. These may in turn affect his expertise. Often, the most difficult problems in doing business in foreign countries is not in the technical know-how or in the special skills involved, but in the understanding of the culture, its value system, its work attitudes, and its business structure. Some expat "representatives" have caused embarrassment to their company and their country by behaving in a boorish manner. When businessmen (and their families) show an insensitivity to the customs and attitudes of the people of the host country, it causes companies to lose business, "face" and friends.

However, much of the expat's "insensitive" behaviour is not due to callousness or maliciousness on his part; it usually happens because he has not been adequately prepared or instructed in what to expect of the local work conditions. He is often unaware that there *are* differences that he must learn to cope with. For example, the businessman in Malaysia who sits back and puts his feet up on his desk in front of his Malay counterpart does not realize that he has caused a personal offence against his co-worker. He does not understand that he has gravely insulted him. One should never show the soles of one's feet to a Malay.

Often, the expat businessman has no one to turn to for advice and information that can demystify cultural differences for him. The Asian will not take it on himself to tell the Westerner these things because (i) he may feel that his etiquette is universally understood and common to all people, or (ii) he would not want to embarrass him by pointing out his errors.

Of course, the knowledge of cultural differences should not be at the expense of professional expertise. In the words of one oil company manager in Southeast Asia: "Don't send me a specialist on Southeast Asia who is curious about the oil business, send me an oil man who is curious about Southeast Asia." What is important is that the expat should be aware of cultural differences, learn about them, and be sensitive to them.

(b) *Stranger Anxiety:* The expat often experiences distress in his own inability to cross the cultural curtain. Some expats do try very hard, and they experience difficulty from always being the "foreigner" in a society where everyone knows just what to do and how to do it except the foreigner. This "strangerness" is often a problem for exasperated expats. They know that they will always be the "stranger", no matter how much they try to understand. Rudyard Kipling's "Stranger" explains this distress:

The Stranger within my gate,
He may be true or kind,
But he does not talk my talk—
I cannot feel his mind.
I see the face and the eyes and the mouth,
But not the soul behind.

The men of my own stock
They may do ill or well,
But they tell the lies I am wonted to,
And they are used to the lies I tell;
And we do not need interpreters
When we go to buy and sell.

The stranger within my gate,
He may be evil or good,
But I cannot tell what powers control—
What reasons sway his mood;
Nor when the Gods of his far-off land
May repossess his blood.

Another problem of living in a foreign culture is being a part of an ethnic minority where it is always the expat who must adjust and not the others!

(c) *Foreign Enterprise:* Expat firms not only have normal competition to contend with, they also face the handicap of operating as "foreign" enterprises. The most important trademark of corporations is not only the competence of their employees, but their conduct. How expats treat local employees can make the difference between the success or failure of the foreign operation.

Some advice for the inexperienced expat entrepreneur!
"You are at the mercy of the foreign businessman until you learn the ropes for yourself!" This is very good advice from one expert expat in Singapore! Doing business in Southeast Asia is like doing business in another world. There are subtleties that the Western businessman would never dream of, for example, paying lower-ranking employees before higher-ranking employees could cause a minor disaster in the office. There has been no published work on business ethics and problems in Singapore and Malaysia that I am aware of, so the expat must learn the hard way, through experience— that often comes too late to prevent major disasters! Here are a few points that expats themselves would like to pass on to the Newcomer:

1 Be aware that there are differences in the business structure.
2 Ask local businessmen in your office to explain how things should be done in the Asian manner.
3 Ask Old-Timer expat businessmen to explain what to do and what not to do.
4 Smile a lot.
5 In the field, always speak to the foreman, or who you think is the most immediate supervisor.
6 Do not make obscene gestures to local workmen — i.e., "the bird", smacking fist against open hand, etc., because the local may walk off the job.
7 Never shout at or "cuss" local workers.
8 Never say anything against their father or mother, i.e., "You son of a b____!"
9 Pay employees through the foreman.
10 Always negotiate—bargain. Not negotiating high enough is the biggest mistake.

11 Never discuss business immediately, spend at least 45 minutes in pleasantries first.

12 Always offer tea at first, not drinks. If the businessman is westernized, then you can offer drinks.

13 It's wise to talk about: food, compliments to Singapore and Malaysia and their governments; it is not wise to talk about personal things and private family matters.

14 Business ethics:
    (a) Westerners like to get to the point immediately. Easterners like formality. Cleverness is admired. They send in the second team first. They can always come back and say that Father said no!
    (b) Never negotiate business in one day, three days is about normal. Time means a different thing here! The first day may be a dinner—at the dinner, no business is discussed. (There may be 12 courses if it is a good contract!)

15 The Eastern business is often a family concern — they don't sack anyone!

2 Problems with Wives

Most of the expat's problems in living in a foreign culture are not personal and business ones; they are, oddly enough, problems with the inability of the wife and children to "settle in". Personnel managers in Southeast Asia have said that when an expat wishes to leave his assignment before his tour of duty is up, it is usually because of family pressure from the wife and children. The overseas wife plays a much more crucial role in the success or failure of her husband's occupation as an expat than she does in his occupation at home. When the wife cannot adjust, family problems spill over into the business life of the expatriate.

It is important that the expat husband be aware of this fact. He should not be taken up so much with the excitement of his job that he neglects this crucial aspect of his wife's role in living and working in an alien society. If husbands devote all

A GUIDE FOR EXPATS 199

their attention and energy to their jobs, marital crises may erupt, and business problems multiply. If the husband travels a great deal (and many husbands in Singapore and Malaysia do), this can add additional stress on the wife who is already feeling lonely because she may have left adult children and grandchildren at home. One expat wife says: "My biggest problem is that I never see my husband any more, and the children never see their father." When a man travels a great deal, he can make it up to his family by being aware that it is hard on them, by understanding their feelings; and by improving the quality of the time he spends with them when he is not travelling.

A man can do much to help his wife by:
(a) Giving her more emotional support than he has ever given her before.
(b) Not taking for granted her efforts to ease the family into the new environment. He should appreciate, praise and encourage any efforts she makes to help the family settle in.
(c) By encouraging family participation in learning about the new culture and its people. He should set the norm as the head of the household in showing respect and consideration for the people in the host society.

3   Some Other Problems Mentioned by Men
As mentioned before, the expat men really have few problems in living the expat life-style. Some of these problems are:
(a) SEPARATION FROM FAMILIES. One expat explains: "My biggest problem is that the larger part of my family is far away." (88 per cent of the men surveyed mentioned this problem. In fact, the percentage of men mentioning this problem was higher than the percentage of women!)
(b) LONELINESS. One expat says: "There is not much chance to make close friends here. We are on a two-year contract, and, as everyone knows, we'll be leaving soon."

(c) Few men (only 9 per cent) mentioned having personal problems.
(d) Several expats mentioned "being away from all the latest changes, news, music and activities of home" as a problem. Many say they are "losing touch with their own culture".
(e) One expat wag finds his most serious problem to be "mildew"!

On the whole, the men seem to be quite happy with the opportunities the expat life has to offer for creative work, job satisfaction, new ideas, experience, seeing how work is done in other countries, and the "opportunities the expat life provides for living a richer, fuller and more exciting life!"

B   Women

The life-style of the expat woman changes dramatically when she moves into a foreign country. The expat family often finds itself living in the upper or middle-upper classes of the society, rather than the comfortable middle class of the old environment. As a wife, the expat woman in Singapore and Malaysia performs most of the duties that she did at home, but these duties are performed in a different physical, social and cultural setting. Unlike her husband, she has no smooth transition from her "job" at home to her "job" in the new environment. She also has no one to help ease this transition for her. At home, there may have been a big separation of home life and work life. In Singapore and Malaysia, this difference is likely to shrink. She often finds herself much more involved in her husband's role in the corporation. She may be caught up in a whirl of entertaining, hostessing, and socializing, as part of her functions as an expat wife. Some wives may enjoy this, while others find it painful.

Another change in her life-style is that her behaviour is no longer a matter of private or family concern. What she does reflects on her husband, his company, and her country. With all these basic differences in mind, the wife also has to contend with many other problems that affect her life as an expat. One survey of expat women identifies some of the most pressing personal problems of the average expatriate women.

1   *Separation from family, adult children, grandchildren and friends.* This problem was mentioned most frequently by expat women (74 per cent of those surveyed) living in Singapore and Malaysia. Leaving behind adult children, grandchildren, family and friends is a source of pain to the expat wife. They might have formed the nucleus of her life while in the old environment. One expat expresses grief: "The most serious disadvantage of the expat life is the separation from dear ones, especially family when they are in trouble or have any illness 12,000 miles away."

2   *The second biggest problem mentioned: "The husband travels too much."* The expat wife often has to survive long periods of loneliness while her husband travels. Itinerant fathers and husbands are common in Singapore and Malaysia. Some husbands spend up to 60 per cent of the year "out of town". Many of the husbands in the off-shore drilling business are home only one or two weeks out of the month. The wife is left to cope with the responsibility of the household and the discipline of the children for long periods of time. She has to learn how to make decisions alone.

3   *The next problem mentioned is the loss of the wife's identity.* Some quotes from expat wives on this problem: 'I miss my financial independence . . . I can't work here, and I left a very fulfilling job at home." "I can't finish my schooling here; I only need a few more credits to finish my law degree, but it's not possible." Many of the expat wives are highly qualified educationally: 30 per cent have finished high school; 32 per cent have at least one to three years of college; and 38 per cent have finished college and some have gone on to higher degrees. The inability of expat women to work at fulfilling and stimulating

occupations or to continue the course of their education causes many problems for the expat wife in Singapore and Malaysia.

These problems are aggravated by the amount of leisure time that the average expat wife has. She often has more household help than she would have in her own home (79 per cent of the expats said that they had more household help abroad than they did at home). Women often have servants, cooks, drivers and gardeners. They may take over many of the traditional duties of the woman's pre-expat life. While this may give her more freedom, it may also give her a loss of prestige and a feeling of uselessness. She may have more boredom to cope with. She may be exposed to more superficiality in her daily life. Since she is not ordinarily allowed to work or study in Singapore and Malaysia, she may have problems in making effective use of her leisure hours. One expat wife says: "A wife needs to feel worthwhile; living here, I do not feel like I am performing my normal role." Many expat women are used to being independent; to working hard; to using their minds; to pursuing their own interests, hobbies, studies and career. In Singapore and Malaysia, the expat wife often has to figure out ways to cope with "nothing to do!" This problem is often difficult for the expat husband to comprehend! "Why are you complaining, you've got it so good!" is a frequent remark made by the expat husband. However, many expat wives would like to see their husbands sitting around with time, talent and energy— and nowhere to go with it!

4   *Running a household is mentioned as being a problem for 53 per cent of the women who took part in the survey.* In spite of modern living conditions and household help many women must adjust to all the daily frustrations that have to do with setting up house in an Asian society *where time is relative!* The Asians do not conceive of time

in the same way that Westerners do. Everything has its own "time" and some things cannot be hurried! A typical quote is heard from one expat wife: "The man was supposed to be here last Friday to repair the air-conditioner; I'm having a dinner party tonight (a week from last Friday), and he still has not come!" In the words of another expat: "The wife has to learn Oriental Patience!"

5   *Problems with servants is another headache for expat wives,* but not in the way that most would think! Her biggest problem with servants is "how to handle them"! How indeed for the egalitarian and independent expat wife. She sometimes never learns how to establish the mistress-*amah* relationship that the locals take for granted. "How can I lie on the sofa and read while the *amah* is working? It's better to go out shopping while she is here." (However, the expat wife soon gets used to having servants, and often finds that she can't do without them.)

Only 27 per cent of the expats surveyed said that they had problems with the quality of their servants. This is probably more a reflection of the excellent quality of household help in Singapore and Malaysia than of the expat's ability to "handle servants".

6   Some other problems mentioned by women:
   (a) *Adjusting to the physical and cultural differences in Singapore and Malaysia* (98 per cent) Women are more severely hit by culture impact than their husbands. Not only do they have more difficulty in coping with the personal problems of expatriate living, but they also have to cope with the cultural adjustment with little or no help from anyone. In spite of the importance of the expat wife in the family's successful adjustment, she is often ignored when it comes to orientation of any kind. It's worse

for the women when husbands simply don't understand why the wife should experience difficulty.
Many of the women surveyed said that they had to
depend on advice from their *amahs* to demystify
cultural differences in Singapore and Malaysia for
them!

(b) *Loss of their own cultural identity*
(c) *Family problems* (45 per cent)
(d) *Personal problems* (37 per cent)
(e) *Problems with children* (37 per cent)
(f) *Problems with marriage* (30 per cent)
(g) *Business problems* (7 per cent)

As we have seen, the wife often has many more cultural
problems than the husband. In addition to the expat life-style
problems she faces, she also knows that the family's success
in adapting to the new culture falls on her shoulders. If she
makes a happy and successful adjustment, the husband and
children will follow suit! If she fails to adjust, the whole
family will suffer.

Some advice for the expat wife

(a) Be especially creative and inventive in finding ways to
maintain your sense of dignity and purposefulness. Keep
busy and cheerful. Realize you must make the most of
your life in a foreign culture. Think of how all your friends
back home are living the daily "rat race"; and think of how
you are seeing new ways of life, how you have an opportunity to do and experience things that most of the people
at home will never have the chance to do! Think of your
experience in a foreign country as a college education
without the pain and misery of taking exams! Develop a
positive attitude that will infect the rest of the family.

(b) Here is an excerpt from a letter written by an expat
teenager to his friend at home (in the middle of winter):
"It was just another average day, nothing much! I'm
sitting here on the porch drinking an iced soda and

watching a red and orange sunset. We spent the day water-skiing and then all stopped at the West Coast for chilli crabs! We went to Tioman last week for the school holidays and I lost my chain while I was skin-diving but the water's so clear that we found it right away." Learn something from your teenagers—they find good in everything! Learn about the culture and customs in Singapore and Malaysia, and teach what you learn to your husband and children. Share what you learn with other expat wives. Help them to appreciate the wonders of an alien culture. Don't stay alone, and don't dwell on your problems.

(c) Be *aware* of the problems in the new culture, and then figure out ways to solve them. *Awareness* is the key to survival!

(d) Set up your home as quickly as possible. Make an easy transition for the husband and children. Create a safe harbour for them.

(e) Take stock of your personal life. Read and improve yourself as a person. Intensify your faith. Psychologists have seen that people with a deep spiritual commitment are ordinarily more mature than others.

(f) Learn to like and accept yourself. Be generous with yourself. Forgive yourself for shortcomings. When you find that you like and accept yourself, you will like and accept other people and their cultures.

(g) Do not restrict your relationships to expats. Make friends with locals too—on an equal-status basis.

(h) Do try to work or attend classes here. Check with the Ministry of Labour to see if you have a special talent that can be used in Singapore or Malaysia.

(i) Do volunteer your help. The expat schools, the local blind school, the Samaritans, etc., are always in need of help from skilled people.

C Children

Children, as well as adults, suffer from many of the problems of the expatriate life. Young children and teenagers too, suffer most when the family is not emotionally healthy and stable. A loving and supportive family life is the most important aspect of a child's adjustment. Children's problems often reflect the problems of their parents. A happy, well-adjusted mother is the key to happy, well-adjusted children. A kind and loving husband is the key to a happy, well-adjusted mother. Children can cope with any difficulties when they know that they are loved deeply for themselves, and that they are accepted for who they are.

Here are some problems as reported by expat teens.

1 PERSONAL PROBLEMS IN ORDER OF FREQUENCY MENTIONED

(a) *Missing old friends and making new friends.* As with adults, making new friends and leaving old friends is one of the most difficult things about the expatriate life for the majority of expat teenagers. The expat teenager may be at an age where he has made close emotional attachments outside his family for the first time in his life. Learning to love, and then leaving loved ones behind, perhaps never to see them again, cause grief and pain. Some teenagers try to avoid this pain by refusing to make close attachments. One says: "I really like Mary, but it was no use asking her out and starting something. I know that I'll be going home to college this summer and she will be going on to another country."

(b) *Adjusting to a new culture and new living conditions.* Teenagers report that culture impact is another one of their biggest problems. New habits to learn, new behavioural expectations, new customs, new people and new ways of eating, speaking and living are all problems of "culture impact". These are problems that every expatriate must eventually face and come to terms with if a successful cultural adjustment is to be made. These cultural problems are compounded by the lack of information available for teenagers. The expat communities, the schools and the expat embassies sadly neglect this crucial aspect of life in an overseas country. Teenagers are generally left on their own to try and work out these problems. The expat schools offer little in the way of cross-cultural classes. As a result of a lack of information and a lack of cross-cultural contact with local people, teenagers often retreat from cultural problems by clumping together with other teenagers of their own kind and removing themselves from contact with the local community. Few teenagers report having more than two to three local friends. It is the same with their parents.

Ethnocentrism is a common problem among expat teenagers. From the results of surveys conducted by this writer a low level of tolerance for the different ethnic groups in Singapore and Malaysia has been reported by teenagers who have never been exposed to cross-cultural classes and close cross-cultural contact. (About 29 per cent of these teenagers expressed tolerant attitudes.) Conversely, when teenagers have been able to take classes in the customs and culture of Singapore and Malaysia, and have had an opportunity to visit with and make friends with local people, their tolerance level has been tripled. (About 90 per cent of these teenagers expressed tolerant attitudes.)

The expatriate communities could do much to help teenagers adapt to the local culture by providing more of these cultural classes that deal with the habits, the language, the customs, the literature, the religions, the attitudes and the courtesies of Singapore and Malaysia.

(c) *School problems and social life.* The third biggest problem that teenagers fall victim to has to do with coping with a new school and a new type of social life. Being a new kid in a new school in a new country in a new culture is not easy. It takes courage and a lot of emotional support from parents. School work may suffer as a young expat is taken out of one school system and transplanted into another. A teenager may have just learned how to cope with the intricacies of one math system, when he suddenly finds that he has to unlearn what he knows and relearn a new procedure.

Some expat teenagers report that the challenge of a new school helps them to do better because they try harder. As one teenager explains: "When you come into a new school system, you try harder because you don't want the others to think that you are dumb! No one knows you, you have a new and fresh start, you don't have to live down any poor reputation that you might have had before."

The social life of teenagers here depends on their acceptance into the established system. Some teenagers report that it is difficult to penetrate the school cliques that have already been formed. On the whole, teenagers say that their social life here is better than in their home country because they rely more on each other for mutual support. Sixty-two per cent felt closer to their friends here than to their friends at home.

(d) *Losing touch with their own country and culture.* Many felt that losing touch with the familiarity of their own culture, food, music, activities, social life, health care, and environment was a problem for them.

(e)   *Problems with parents.* These problems were low on the list of priorities for expat teenagers. Only two per cent felt that their relationships with their parents were worse than they were before the expat life. Four per cent said that they had never been close to their parents to begin with. All the rest said that their relationships were just as good, or even better since they began living the expat life.

Teenagers are philosophical about expatriate living and family life. Fifty-four per cent felt that while they believed teenagers had more adjustment problems than parents did, it was only because teenagers had more particular problems in general to cope with, and they would experience them in any type of culture. They actually felt that it was more difficult for the parents because: "Kids are used to new things; they don't know anything different. Parents are older and more set in their ways; leaving home for them is a bigger thing because they are not used to change." Another teenager speaks for a majority of teenagers when he says: "I think that mothers have the most problems. They have to leave all their friends behind. Sure, they can make friends here, but it's not like having the same old friends they've had for thirty years." Another teenager says: "Fathers like it here, they have more responsibility in their jobs, and they like the challenges." Another philosophical teenager comments: "My father travels a lot, and it's hard on my mom; but I can change all the fuses in the house, and I can stop the washing machine from leaking."

(f)   *Not being able to have part-time jobs.* Teenagers, as well as their mothers, are not allowed to work in Singapore and Malaysia without work permits. Twenty-nine per cent of the teenagers stated that they were definitely unhappy about not having a part-time or week-end job. One teenager expresses it this way: "At home, I had a week-end job, and I was able to pay my own way on dates. It's sort of degrading to have to ask your parents for a hand-out every week. It's like going back in time a few steps." Another says: "If I was home right now, I'd have a few hundred dollars in my pocket because of all the snow-storms they've been having. There would be a lot of drive-ways to clean out. When I work for my money, I feel better, I appreciate it more."

(g) *Not being able to drive here.* Legal age for driving is eighteen years. Many teenagers miss the freedom of being able to drive themselves to school, and on errands and dates. They depend on taxis (which are plentiful and cheap) and buses.

II   OTHER PROBLEMS OF TEENAGERS

(a) *Drugs.* Drugs can be a danger for teenagers in Singapore and Malaysia. These countries are close to the Golden Triangle, and drugs can filter through even the most vigilant of authorities. There are severe penalties for drug use, and there is a death penalty for drug dealers. Drug use can cause much more serious repercussions in this part of the world than they can in other parts of the world.

A teenager who uses drugs here brings disgrace to his country, his father's company, his family and his expatriate community. He is subject to a jail term and/or deportation. Parents are warned to do everything in their power to prevent their teenagers from coming into contact with any type of drug.

One teenager expresses it like this: "You'd have to be a fool to use drugs here!"

(b) *Alcohol.* The legal age for drinking here is eighteen

years. Teenagers have more access to legal drinking in Singapore and Malaysia than they would have in their own home country because they often look older than their Asian counterparts. Parents are warned that drinking can become a problem for their teenaged children.

On the whole, teenagers are flexible and positive about the experience of expat life. They have the ability to see the best parts of it. One teenager says: "At home, everybody is going to the football games, but I've learned how to survive in the jungle, climb Mt. Kota Kinabalu, and how to tap rubber. I can speak Malay, and I can bargain in shops better than my parents can!" Another teenager reports: "I travelled all through India, Nepal, France, Germany and England with two other friends on our way home last year. We had to take care of our own passports, arrange our flights and handle all the details. Not many kids back home would be able to do all that."

One last word from a teenager that sums up the teen experience: "Living the way we do doesn't have too many problems really; we learn to build up a tolerance for differences!"

Some advice for parents

(a) Give your child close, warm and loving emotional support.

(b) Involve your child in the decision to make the move. Assign him the responsibility of writing to embassies, travel agencies and tourist boards to gather as much information about the new country and its culture as he can. Have the child share his information with the family and praise him for contributing to the family's under-standing. (This is best done before the move into the new country.)

(c) Take an active part in your child's new school: join the PTA, volunteer to be a room mother or to go on field trips

PLEASURES AND BENEFITS OF EXPAT LIFE

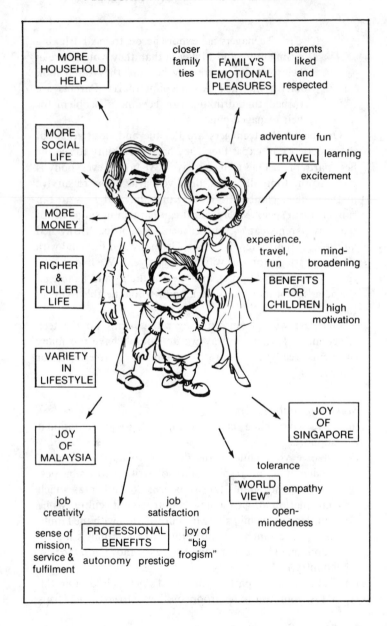

SOME PROBLEMS OF THE PERIPATETIC EXPATS

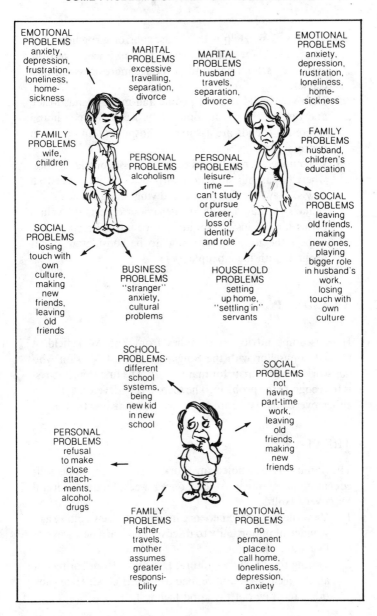

with his class. Help with scouts, cubs or girl-guides. Let your child know that you support him. Encourage your expatriate school board to introduce more cross-cultural classes.

(d) Help your child to meet people and make friends inside and outside the expat community. Keep an open house where his friends are assured of hospitality and a warm welcome.

(e) Encourage your child to sign up for classes outside school, where he can mix and meet with locals, as well as learn a new skill, water skiing, scuba diving, kung fu, etc.

(f) Make sure that your child's behaviour reflects the values of his family, his school and his country. Teach him to respect the local culture, and to be considerate in his dealings with local people.

A FAMILY PLAN

Here is some advice for families from Bob Wakefield, a trained counsellor with the Singapore Baptist Mission who has worked with expats for many years. The first step, he says, is to recognise the problem. The second is to develop a *plan* to either overcome the problem or else try to live with it!

THE PLAN

The family as a whole can work together on some self-education programme. At least once a week, hold a "Cultural Discovery Hour".

1   View the family's experience in living in a new culture as a wonderful opportunity to discover and learn new ways of living and thinking.

2   During this "Family Cultural Discovery Hour" bring out all the feelings you have, bad as well as good. Help each other to draw out the good feelings!

3   Discuss the problem of cultural impact and its causes.
4   Verbalize feelings, bring them up to the surface.
5   Develop a spirit of adventure; discover new foods, see the attraction in living in a unique culture.
6   Discuss ways and means to learn about the new culture:
     (a) Assume the role of "learner" and ask locals to become the "teachers".
     (b) Seek information actively on the do's and don'ts, the whys and the hows. The more you learn, the more the strange will become familiar to you, and the more you will learn to feel comfortable, at ease, and pleased with your new environment!
     (c) Get out and meet the local people.

WHAT ARE SOME OF THE PLEASURES AND BENEFITS OF THE EXPAT LIFE?

1   Families—Parents and Children

One of the most pleasant benefits for families living overseas is the close relationships that develop between parents and children. In one study by Ruth Hill Useem (on "Third-culture Kids" or TCKs)[2] she reports that the overwhelming majority of TCKs (close to 90 per cent) like, respect and feel emotionally attached to their parents. (Note: Expat teenagers in this area have reported a similar closeness to their parents— 94 per cent.)

Some reasons for this:

(a) The high mobility of third-culture families, who usually move every few years, seems to have the effect of bringing individual family members together. They share the common experience of moving into unfamiliar territory and offer each other mutual support in the face of change and strangeness. Parents are often the only people with whom teenagers have a continuing relationship as they move from one location to another.

(b) Families overseas spend more time together than do their home-country counterparts, and the time together is often not taken up with mundane aspects of living. They take more holidays together, and plan more activities together.

(c) Mothers are home managers rather than housewives, because they usually have servants to clean up the spilled milk, make the beds, and cook meals. As one overseas mother said. "It's amazing how pleasant children can be when one is not frantically trying to get supper on, answer the phone, and nag the children to pick up their clothes."

2 Family Closer

Another bonus is that expats often report being closer as a family because of the forces operating in the foreign setting. Anthropologists say that frequently members of a family in a new and strange situation are pulled closer together. The foreign experience tends to heighten family cohesiveness.[3] The anxiety of being a stranger in a strange land can cause people to rely on the family group as a defence. The family members are thrown together and have to rely on each other for mutual support and emotional sustenance. In Singapore and Malaysia however, only 39 per cent of the families surveyed reported feeling closer *as a family*. (This low figure may have resulted because of the highly developed and organized expat communities that exist in Singapore and Malaysia. The typical expat family is not really a stranger in the expat community, though he may be a stranger in the alien society. The family may rely more on the community than on family members for support and sustenance.)

3 Children

Useem also sees TCKs as the people who, as future adults, will be following in their parents' footsteps and fulfilling mediating roles in the increasingly conflictive and inter-dependent global system. The problems of adjustment that TCKs experience offer them valuable experience that helps prepare them for their future roles, which will probably be international. (A recent survey of expat teenagers here revealed that 74 per cent would prefer to travel in their life's work as expats, rather than to stay put in their home country.) In order to qualify for careers in the third culture, these young people are highly motivated to do well in school and to attain college degrees. Many of the expats mentioned this factor in the survey. One expat wife says: "This style of life offers an invaluable experience for our children to learn about other people and other cultures." An expat father says: "One of the greatest benefits that comes from living and working in a foreign culture is the opportunity it gives for expanding the world outlook for the children; it helps to broaden their minds."

4 World View

This mind-broadening aspect of living as an expat spills over into the adult community. The majority of expats have reported a development of tolerance and openmindedness. Successful adjustment to living in a foreign culture; the learning of new languages; the exposure to other people's views, values and life-styles contribute to a cosmopolitan "world-view" that gives both parents and children a deeper understanding of the more important things in life. Of the expats surveyed, 70 per cent said this particular advantage was one of the greatest benefits to living in foreign cultures. One expat man expressed it this way: "You get a whole new perspective on life, and you develop a finer appreciation for other cultures and other people."

5 Travel

Expats also have an opportunity to travel, to see new and exotic places, to experience new things and to live a life of adventure and excitement. One expat wife says: "There are the financial benefits, of course, but I think, more important, you get a chance to see and live as other people do. Seeing the world first-hand is a wonderful thing!" An expat husband says: "Living the expat life offers a better perspective of all cultural values and behaviour. I only wish I had done this twenty years ago." In a survey, 70 per cent of the expat women and 89 per cent of the men said that travel, adventure and excitement were some of the greatest pleasures to be had in living this style of life. Fifty-three per cent of teens mentioned the benefits of travel and adventure as being some of their greatest pleasures too.

6 Professional

There are many professional benefits for the expat male. Expat men say: "There is greater job status" (47 per cent of all males surveyed reported this factor); "more prestige"; "more job satisfaction"; "more opportunity for creative work"; "more job autonomy"; "more responsibility". Some men experience a deep sense of pleasure and service in their work: "I had a sincere desire to help others to develop, that is why I came here!" Several other men mentioned a sense of mission and fulfilment in their work. One expat wife says: "My husband loves his work here, he hopes to do more for his company here than he can do at home." Of the male inter-viewees, 73 per cent said that they came to work in Southeast Asia to improve their professional positions, or because of a sense of mission and service.

Anthropologists speak of the joy of "Big Frogism" as being an important factor in keeping expats happy overseas. One expat explains it this way: "I have to know every detail of the operation. At home there would be four or five men in the same office doing the same thing that I am doing here. I wouldn't have the control that I have here. There's so much satisfaction in being in charge of everything. You can do something and know that you did it."

7 Variety

Another emotional benefit is the constant variety in the life-style. Many expats mentioned this fact in the survey. "You get out of a rut and you avoid humdrum." "You have the opportunity to make a new start." "You can get rid of old habits and make new ones, eating habits for example!" "You have a richer, fuller and more exciting life—there's something new every day!" "There's more change: new cuisine, new cultures, new ways of doing and seeing things."

8   **Besides all these intangible benefits, there are also some tangible ones:**

(a) *Money:* The expat often makes more money than his contemporaries at home. (However, this may not hold true for very long if rising taxes don't come to a halt!) One expat says: "We have an opportunity to save money for our children's education and for our retirement!" Seventy-two per cent of the expats surveyed said that they made more money as expatriates than they did at home.

(b) *Homes:* Twenty-eight per cent of the expats surveyed said that they had a better house here than they did at home.

(c) *Household help*: Seventy-nine per cent of the expats said that they had more household help than they did at home, and this, they said, gave them more leisure time and a greater freedom to participate in community service, hobbies and sports. Several expats mentioned the easy access to sailing, water-skiing, tennis, squash, and several other sports. However, one expat said that one of his biggest problems was not being able to play golf here. (There are golf courses, but many of them have a long waiting list, or they are too outrageously expensive to join.)

(d) *Social life:* Forty-nine per cent of the expats surveyed said that they had a more active social life in Singapore and Malaysia than they did at home.

The Pleasures of Expatriate Life as Reported by Teenagers

The teenagers experience pleasure a little differently than do their parents. Their greatest pleasures, in order of frequency:

(a) *Increased world-view*. The overwhelming majority of teenagers felt that an enhanced world view was their greatest pleasure in living the expat life. Learning about new people and places, broadening their mind, the development of maturity that comes with the expansion of ideas, seeing new ways of life, exposure to cultural differences, personal interactions with people from different cultures, learning new ways of doing and thinking, personal development and personal growth were mentioned most frequently by teenagers in a recent survey.

(b) *Experience*. Challenging and exciting experiences were next on the teenager's list of pleasures.

(c) *Travel*. The opportunity to see the world first-hand was the third greatest pleasure mentioned.

(d) *Excitement*. Something new all the time was another pleasure frequently mentioned.

(e) The following pleasures were also mentioned, but they were low on the teenagers' list of priorities:

  1 Money
  2 Opportunity
  3 Good living
  4 Beer

The Joy of Singapore and Malaysia

Besides all the benefits of being an expat, the teenagers had a lot more to say about the pleasure of living in Singapore and Malaysia. Their quotes follow:

Singapore: "The greatest benefit of being an expat is that you get to travel; you experience new cultures, new people and new ideas." "You meet people from all over the world and the fun of living in Singapore is great too!" "In Singapore, there are lots of taxis—if you can't get the car from your folks, taxis are always cheap and available." "You never have to worry about the climate here, it's always warm; you can go water-skiing a lot." "You can take a girl out for a date to a food stall for satay and a cold beer (legal age in Singapore is 18) and it can be really cheap—about three or four US dollars would cover the whole thing." "If you go to a good restaurant at one of the big hotels, they give you the red-carpet service, and it really impresses your girl." "The service is great at the hotels; we stayed in one before we moved into our apartment, and they really treat you nice; the service is excellent, and the maids clean up your room when you go out." "The night life is really good, you can get anywhere in town and then walk home at night. *You don't have to worry about getting mugged either!*" "There's really a lot to do here, you can get a group together and hire a boat to take you out to an island for the day."

Malaysia: "It's not so small, there are a lot of big states that you can go to—you can get in the car and drive without worrying about bringing passports, etc." "Kuala Lumpur has lots of advantages—a lot of night life." "There's a good and cheap train system that goes all over Malaysia." "Really nice coastal and tropical islands! Good beaches like Penang and Tioman." "They have a great national park and you can see wild life there—the Taman Negara is beautiful!" "Malaysia is quiet and peaceful—the air is fresh and smells good out in the country." "There is a wide range of scenery: you can go to the beach, go mountain climbing, go camping; and you can see a lot of historical monuments!" "You have greater chances to meet more local people in Malaysia—*you meet people who go all out for you!*" "There's a lot of space in Malaysia—you can get away from the big crowds and the city noises! Some parts of Malaysia are nice and cool—you can get a change of pace from the hot and steamy tropics."

Before we leave this section, we should mention that there are some additional benefits to being an Old-timer expat. Old-timers get the hang of the expatriate life-style, and soon learn how to cope with the problems that accompany it.

1   Old-timers reported two and a half times less problems than First-timers did in the following areas: personal, family, marriage, children, social life, business, money, household and servants.

2   Nearly twice as many Old-timer women than First-timer women reported that their families were closer since living the expat life.

3   Three times more Old-timer wives mentioned "A love for travel" as being a motive for travelling than First-timer wives did.

4   Fifty-three per cent of Old-timer women said that it was much easier to adjust to a move to a foreign country because they had lived as an expatriate before!

NOTES FOR POTENTIAL EXPATRIATES

Before deciding on living the life of an expatriate, the family must consider carefully the problems and benefits that are reported by the expats living in Singapore and Malaysia. Each member of the family should be aware of the pleasure and pain that accompany the life-style of the expatriate; *it is easier to do this before leaving home!*

The family should keep in mind that a move to a foreign country will not ordinarily patch up a shaky marriage, or bring together a family that is not close to begin with. A stable marriage often makes the difference between success and failure of the overseas experience.

Children should be consulted on their feelings about making a move to an alien society. However, it is a good idea to let them know that many expat teenagers report an easier adjustment to the expat life-style than their parents do.

Don't decide on the move unless the whole family agrees whole-heartedly. It is especially important that the mother of the family be a hundred per cent behind the move. The mother plays a crucial role in the success or failure of the entire family's adjustment, and also a crucial role in the success or failure of the husband's role as an expatriate employee.

If both parents have a "travel-bug" nature then chances of success are good! A remark often heard by the successful expat wife is: "I just like this life—I like the travel— it's fun!"

There are many other things that a potential expatriate must consider before making a major decision to relocate his family to a foreign country:

1 *The job design of the overseas position and length of stay.*
2 *The location of the country, and general information on its practical aspects,* i.e., political structure, health conditions, climate, education for children.
3 *Selling or renting your house* (Many expats are shocked to find that they can no longer afford the same type of house that they sold prior to moving overseas. Being out of their home country for several years keeps them out of touch with the spiralling cost of housing.)
4 *Taxes* — both in the home country and the foreign country. Expats should be very familiar with the tax laws.
5 *Company policy on transportation of household goods,* mechanics and allowances for shipping furniture or replacement of such. Housing arrangements, rents, and allowances.
6 *Travel and home-leave arrangements.*
7 *Health precautions,* legal advice, availability of shopping centres, physicians, etc.

(Note: "LIVING IN SINGAPORE", put out by the American Association of Singapore can answer many of these questions for potential expatriates. This book can be obtained from the American Association of Singapore c/o The American Club, 21 Scotts Road, Singapore 0922.)

Notes for business organizations

What can be done to ensure that (1) the multinational organizations choose the right man to be an expert expat and (2) everything possible is done to give him and his family the help needed so they can be successful expats?

1 **What can be done to ensure that the multinational organization chooses the right man?**

    (a) The company must choose the man who first of all has the best professional and technical skills.

    (b) The company must then look at his personality. The man must be chosen for his *cultural empathy,* i.e., "the skill he has to understand the inner logic and coherence of other ways of life, plus the restraint not to judge them as bad because they are different from his own ways. A certain involvement in alien ways—short of "going native"—may become the most effective device for building a personal, business, and social bridge from one culture to another."[4]

        Besides cultural empathy, the man must be chosen for the degree of his curiosity, interest in the alien culture, his sense of humour, his adaptability, flexibility, his sense of "wanderlust or travel-bugness" and most of all for his "tolerant personality".[5] (Note: Psychological tests should reveal this "tolerant personality".)

(c) If possible, the company should choose a bachelor! If the person chosen is married, the company must look at the stability of his home life. Many overseas problems are caused because of family problems. The family which is not stable at home is likely to become more unstable overseas. Stable and healthy family relationships can make the difference between success and failure in the overseas assignments.

(d) The company must then choose the man's *wife!* Many studies on overseas expatriates have found that the wife plays a crucial role in the success or failure of the husband's mission in the foreign culture. One expat personnel director here says: "In my experience, I have found that over 50 per cent of the problems the man has in his work are directly caused by the inability of the wife to adjust. When she is not happy, she presses him to pull out!" This is confirmed by the studies of expats in many parts of the world. Ruth Hill Useem, in studying the American family in India, reported that when wives cannot adjust they apply pressure on the husband to leave his position, be reassigned somewhere else, or else they leave their husbands. She says that "fumbling" wives are burdensome to their husbands and the organization sponsoring their husbands. They place the blame for their unhappiness on the company; *they complain long, loud and bitterly, and they are disruptive to the rest of the wives.*[6]

Because of the crucial role the wife plays in the success or failure of the family's adjustment, and the role that she plays in the success or failure of the husband's role, there have been many attempts to try and predict the type of wife that would make the most successful expat wife. There has not been much success in this endeavour. However, through interviews, surveys, and observation, we may be able to offer advice on how to predict one type of successful expat wife.

The Travel Bug

In investigating the successful expat wife, it has been observed that those most successful in adapting are those who derive the most pleasure from living in alien cultures. They love "travel" for itself; they are curious, they love new experiences; *they love to try new and exotic foods;* they like to meet new people; they read a lot; they are adventurous and they have a direct interest in the foreign culture. These women generally have a cheerful and positive nature; they are enthusiastic and *they seem to be inordinately healthy.* Few of them report even getting a cold.

These women have had the wanderlust spirit from as far back as they can remember. They would choose to travel, even if they weren't married! They have a long history of travelling before their husbands' assignment oveseas. One of these successful adaptors says: "I just love people. I've travelled all my life; I went to Sweden when I was only 5 years old. This piqued my interest in travelling, and I've been travelling, or wanting to, ever since. When my husband was asked if he wanted to work here, he accepted without even asking me. He knew I would jump at the chance!"

This type of wife makes a successful expat wife. She infects her family with the joy of living in a foreign culture. She supports her husband in his work, and she helps her family to settle in easily. This type of wife often turns out to be a happy "Cosmopolitan".

2   **What can the company do to ensure that everything possible is done to give the expat and his family the help they need so they can be successful expats?**

    (a) *Before leaving home:* Some very good advice is quoted here from Frank L. Acuff, Corporate Employee Relations Supervisor, J. Ray McDermott and Co., Inc., New Orleans, Louisiana: "Advice, training, cultural orientation and preparation are essential to the success of the man's overseas assignment. Advice about health precautions, legal advice on Law of Domicile, orientation to company policies, kidnapping precautions, *social structure of the foreign culture (i.e., customs, traditions, manners, habits, attitudes, beliefs, etc., as well as the physical orientation,* shopping, physicians, etc., are needed in the employee's arsenal of information in order to ensure the best chances for a smooth transfer. Unlike the other levels of awareness, i.e., job designs, taxes, salary, travel arrangements, etc. this information is not apt to be solicited by the employee. In most cases, the company must initiate awareness, and stress the specific details of these factors. *For international transfers, fully informing employees of these factors can mean the difference between high and marginal productivity, retention or quit, and corporate gains and losses.* Until these needs are met, the employee will not be free to develop his capabilities. The company must take the responsibility for stressing these factors since only in this way can it ensure that it has transferred a well-oriented employee who is free to concentrate on activities of mutual benefit."[7]

    (b) *After arrival in the foreign country:* The expat and his family should be given practical information and advice on cultural orientation. Only 16 per cent of the expats surveyed here reported that their companies had provided them with assistance in how to adjust to the physical and cultural conditions of Singapore and Malaysia. Classes, training, lectures, books and guidance are important in helping the employee and his family settle in and adjust to the differences. Cultural orientation also develops an appreciation for the culture and makes for better cross-cultural relations. It raises the tolerance level and improves the expat's attitudes towards the local people. The effects of cross-cultural education are enhanced when the company sanctions and encourages it.

Besides cultural orientation, orientation on local business practices and company structure, work attitudes and work ethics of the local country, chain-of-command, authority, formality, and information about the rules that regulate the everyday business practices in the foreign country should be given. An example of the type of help the expat needs can be seen under: Some Advice for the Inexperienced Expat Entrepreneur, page 197.

The results of the failure of foreign governments and international companies to prepare their employees properly for life in a foreign culture are many:

1   Companies should be aware that cultural diplomacy can make the difference between the success or failure of their operations in a foreign culture. They must be sure that their people are equipped not only with special job skills, but also with the sensitivity to handle cultural differences. They should realize that social blunders and cultural foot-in-mouth disease cost them time, money and prestige.

2   Expats may not be able to adjust properly and may then desire to return to their home before their term is up. This is very costly to multinational corporations.

3   Families may suffer additional problems because of their

inability to cope with the additional strain of adjusting to a foreign culture. Marital problems, drug and alcohol problems, ineffective business dealings, personal and emotional problems increase when an employee is not well oriented in all aspects of his new assignment.

4   Little understanding or friendship can develop between different countries if foreign government or business "representatives" fail to convey an image of friendship and respect towards the foreign culture they are living and working in.

Companies must also be aware that executives, technicians and their families must adjust to living in a foreign culture or their training and expertise may not be effective. The executive and technician are both automatically persons of prestige in a foreign country. They both should be given orientation at both ends (home country and foreign country) so that they can adapt with some success to the new environment.

One last thing that may or may not be important to multinational corporations is the fact that executives and technicians carry the tools that make for economic development. The business world has the potential to take the lead in bringing international peace and friendship to men of all societies; it is through business that men will come to realize that they share the same world and that all men are brothers. Business and multinational corporations are likely to be non-partisan and internationalistic. Through "money" and "profit", mutual dependence and friendship can be developed. Through shared common business interests and goals multinational corporations can bridge the gap that separates one country from another.

Notes

1 Snodgrass, Lanny, "Adjustments Necessary for Overseas Living", *Singapore American Newspaper,* October 1976, Vol. 18, No. 11, p. 2.

2 Useem, Ruth H., "The American Family in India", The Annals of the American Academy of Political and Social Science, Vol. 368.

3 Cleveland, Mangone and Adams, op. cit.

4 Cleveland, *et al.,* op. cit., p. 136.

5 Allport, op. cit., pp. 407-11.

6 Useem, Ruth H., op. cit., p. 133.

7 Frank L. Acuff, Corporate Employee Relations Supervisor, New Orleans, Louisiana. J. Ray McDermott and Co. Inc., November 1974.

**Other *CULTURE SHOCK!* titles
by Times Books International:**

Culture Shock Burma by Mi Mi Khaing. A many-faceted experience. Cultural attitudes and taboos pervading a proud and sensitive race, in a country cut off from foreign influence for a quarter century. With an essential section on how to time visits for maximum advantage.

Culture Shock Indonesia by Cathie Draine and Barbara Hall. A 'hands-on' guide to interacting with Indonesians at social and business levels. Also, for the first time in this series, how to deal with *reverse* culture shock.

Culture Shock Philippines by Alfredo and Grace Roces. A lively and enjoyable guide to Filipino folkways. With indispensable checklists summarising the do's and don'ts of every conceivable area of interaction, from dating to dealing with officialdom.

Culture Shock Thailand by Robert and Nanthapa Cooper. A thoroughly enjoyable book on Thai culture. The humour and empathy will touch you, the expert analysis and perception impress you. The wit will absolutely put you in stitches!